FINDING FAITH

IN A SKEPTICAL WORLD

CHET GALASKA

TRIAD PRESS
LONGMEADOW, MASSACHUSETTS
2012

Finding Faith in a Skeptical World
Published by Triad Press, Longmeadow, MA

Copyright © 2008, 2012 by C.W. Galaska

Manufactured in the United States of America. All rights reserved. No part of this book may be reproduced in any form or by any electronic or mechanical means including information storage and retrieval systems without permission from the publisher, except by a reviewer, who may quote brief passages in a review.

ISBN 978-0-9816767-0-8
Second Edition, Revised

Author Photograph by Robert Charles Photography.
Cover design by United Writers Press

www.ChristianStandpoint.com

Scripture taken from the HOLY BIBLE, NEW INTERNATIONAL VERSION Copyright © 1973, 1978, 1984 by International Bible Society. The "NIV" and "New International Version" trademarks are registered in the United States Patent and Trademark Office by International Bible Society. Use of either trademark requires the permission of International Bible Society. Used by permission of Zondervan Publishing House. All rights reserved.

Praise for
Finding Faith in a Skeptical World

"*Finding Faith in a Skeptical World* by Chet Galaska is an excellent book for those who are seeking a relationship with God and for those who are looking for answers. We live in a confusing world with mixed messages about Christianity coming to us from all angles. *Finding Faith* helps us to make sense of these mixed messages in an engaging, honest and refreshing way. Read it with an open heart and seriously consider how you might establish and deepen your relationship with God."

— *Ben Rivera* —
Campus Crusade for Christ

"*Finding Faith in a Skeptical World* is one of the most practical, refreshing reads I've come across in a long time...down-to-earth but not condescending...I, for one, plan to give copies to my non-Christian friends..."

— *Kathi Macias* —
Award winning author of more than 20 books, including the best-selling devotional A Moment a Day

---

"Every honest skeptic owes it to himself or herself to read Chet Galaska's *Finding Faith in a Skeptical World*...a critical component in charting an honest journey toward truth."

— *Daryl E. Witmer* —
Christian apologist and Executive Director of the AIIA Institute

---

"*Finding Faith* is a very helpful tool. I highly recommend it to all believers and also as a gift for those you know who are struggling with their faith."

— *Rev. Dr. Samuel J. Hollo* —
Director of "The Carpenter's Workshop"

"*Finding Faith in a Skeptical World* is a wonderful vehicle to help Christians understand their faith and share it with others."

— *Atty. Chuck Crismier* —
Host of the national Christian radio program "Viewpoint"

"*Finding Faith* is an easy to read practical book for the skeptic desiring to grow in their faith while facing the many challenges in the world."

— *Ron Willoughby* —
Executive Director, Springfield Rescue Mission

"*Finding Faith in a Skeptical World* takes troublesome issues and turns them into reasons for belief instead of doubt. I highly recommend it."

—*Pastor Dick Loftus* —
Westfield Evangelical Free Church

"*Finding Faith* takes on the task of defending Christianity in a way that connects with both seekers and those wrestling with current issues of faith."

— *Rev. Earl E. Eisenbach* —
Pastor, Agawam Congregational Church

"*Finding Faith in a Skeptical World* superbly illustrates for the skeptic and the faithful Christian how modern-day men and women can see the hand of God in their everyday lives and how they may reconcile their doubts with the scientific community. I highly recommend it."

— *Rev. Fr. Christopher H. Stamas* —
Pastor, St. George Greek Orthodox Cathedral

Dedication

*This book is dedicated to
my wife Lisa,
my sons Drew and Jon,
and my mom, Virginia.*

Contents

	Preface	vii
1	Jesus Is the Answer	1
2	In the Beginning...There was Doctor Dave	5
3	Philosophy 101	9
4	Who Is Jesus?	15
5	Prayer	19
6	Forgiveness	25
7	Redemption and Salvation	33
8	Satan	39
9	Sin	47
10	Judgment Day	53
11	The Trinity	57
12	Why Do Bad Things Happen?	61
13	War	67
14	The Bible	75
15	Why Are There So Many Different Christian Churches?	85
16	The Crusades, the Inquisition and Other "Christian" Atrocities	91
17	Born Agains	99

18	Christian Charity	105
19	The Christian Walk	109
20	The Prism	113
21	Hypocrisy	117
22	Scientific Perception	121
23	Creation	131
24	Evolution	141
25	A False Choice	151
26	Miracles	153
27	Other Religions and Belief Systems	161
28	The Jews	165
29	Elvis Has Left the Building...or Has He?	171
30	A Final Point to Ponder	175
	Afterword	177
	Acknowledgments	181
	Notes	183
	About the Author	208

Preface

I was an atheist, but became a Christian in my early fifties. It took several years of learning about the faith for me to shed my skepticism and become a believer.

Finding Faith in a Skeptical World covers subjects that once stood between me and faith. As I searched, I found that my skepticism was based on shallow impressions I'd accepted at face value. One by one, troublesome issues were explained and they became reasons for belief instead of doubt.

It was as though I had a scale, with reasons for skepticism on one side and reasons for belief on the other. When I started, there was far more weight on the "skeptical" side, but it gradually shifted and became counterweight on the "belief" side. Eventually, the evidence for faith far outweighed the arguments for disbelief, and the case for faith became overwhelming.

As I searched, I became attuned to news stories about Christianity and realized two things. First, there is a steady supply of people representing themselves as believers who say and do things that are not only non-Christian, but just plain wacky. Second, the media gleefully publicizes these people and happily reports whatever "those crazy Christians" are up to. This misrepresents the faith in a subtle but persistent way that affects what people think about Christianity without their even being aware of it. My purpose is to go back to the basics and explain the faith for what it is, and not what people "think" it is.

Some chapters deal with matters of faith such as prayer, redemption, salvation and sin. Others address issues like Christian hypocrisy, why bad things happen, miracles, and the Christian view of war. Some are about the seemingly contradictory relationship between science and religion that are discussed in chapters on scientific perception, creation, and evolution. Other subjects like the sometimes violent and cruel history of Christianity, "Born Agains" and the Christian view of the Jewish people don't fit neatly into any category. The common denominator is that each addresses an issue that can be misunderstood and create a distorted, negative view of the faith.

This book was written with the intent of providing brief shortcuts for curious unbelievers, those seeking faith, those new to it, and for Christians who may not be familiar with some of the ideas covered. I found the answers by reading, participating in a weekly Bible study group, attending church, going to Sunday School classes, being mentored one-on-one by knowledgeable Christians, and being attuned to the unfair misconceptions our culture surrounds us with. A book like this would have been valuable in helping me come to faith. Since none was available, I wrote one to help others.

I don't represent myself to be a scholar or my explanations to be scholarly. I only wish to share the things I've learned that enabled me to overcome barriers to faith. My hope is that this book will promote a clearer understanding of Christianity by both skeptics and believers – and that some doubters will, like me, genuinely open their minds and examine the faith more deeply on their own.

1
Jesus Is the Answer

What's the Question?

✦✦✦✦✦✦✦✦✦✦✦

Pastor Bob Riedy approached a lectern that was surrounded by rocks of various sizes, configurations and colors. He was dressed in a suit and tie but carried a large burlap bag, the kind farmers use for potatoes or grain.

As he spoke of the burdens people carry, he put one stone after another into the sack. For each episode a new stone was thrown in. Some were small, others larger, and still others large enough to significantly increase the weight of the bag.

- *"When you were six, your best friend deserted you."*
- *"In junior high school classmates made fun of the way you dressed."*
- *"You wanted to be a cheerleader in the worst way but got cut from the team."*
- *"The girl you were going steady with broke up with you."*

The sack became burdensome.

- *"Your marriage foundered over constant arguments about money."*

- *"You said something you wished you could take back, but it was too late."*
- *"You had a miscarriage."*
- *"The workload at your job is overwhelming."*

The bag got heavier.

- *"You have a mortgage, a car payment, two kids and a layoff notice."*
- *"You got divorced."*
- *"Your mom died."*
- *"Your child has a serious illness."*
- *"Drugs and alcohol took over your life."*

The weight was overwhelming and the sack just sat there, draining the strength out of anyone who tried to budge it.

We all have burdens that weigh us down. Some people try to deal with them on their own and become self-absorbed, unhappy, depressed, and maybe even suicidal. Others attend support groups. Television, radio, and self help books offer quick fix advice. Those who can afford it may go to psychiatrists or psychologists. But in the end people are still left with their burdens.

And on top of all this, we're afraid of death. People can have personal ideas about it that may make them comfortable, but deep down they know their musings are just wishful thinking. The uncertainties, apprehensions and fears about the one inevitable fact of life remain untouched.

Christ offers forgiveness, support and eternal life. These are the keys to dealing with our troubles. When we do something we regret, we can come to Jesus, obtain forgiveness and overcome our guilt. This removes stones from the sack. The wisdom that comes from prayerful consideration of issues before we act helps us to make correct decisions that keep burdens from occurring in the first place. This prevents stones from being put in the sack. The promise of eternal life puts our problems into perspective: they're just part of a short life on earth that is merely a prelude to a peaceful everlasting life. This reduces the weight of the remaining stones and removes the sting of death.[1] Altogether, the stresses that are an inescapable part of life become manageable.

Here's the catch. In order for this to work a person must truly believe in Jesus Christ. As products of the 20th and 21st centuries, surrounded by skepticism, this can be hard for us to do. But if we open our minds and overcome our doubts, the peace that comes with faith is ours.

The question is: How can I effectively deal with the pressure, guilt, uncertainty, unhappiness, turmoil, fear, tragedy and other burdens that weigh me down?

The answer is: Jesus Christ.

2

In the Beginning... There was Doctor Dave

The Spark That Ignited Curiosity

In the late winter of 2000, I was in the office of my physician, Dr. David Ballan. As usual, the conversation turned to stress. I found myself working interminably, worrying about business problems, not sleeping well, and getting weary of dealing with it all.

The conversation was typical of most of my visits to him over the past twenty years. But this one turned out to be different, because the good doctor took off his medical "hat" and put on his spiritual one. He told me he taught a class at his church on the subject of handling stress through religious faith, and invited me to attend the next session.

My skepticism about Christianity had been unchecked for thirty years, so I didn't think anything helpful would come out of this. But I attended the classes anyway, out of respect for Dave and curiosity about how he fit into this religious environment.

The class lasted for 10 weeks, and provided biblical insights into how faith can make a positive difference in a person's life.

Surprisingly, Dr. Ballan's Bible-based teachings made logical sense. I still had lots of issues with religion, but my interest was aroused.

I started going to church services and was invited to join a Bible study group. The study group included my physician, a surgeon and an architect who was in charge of the Post Office buildings in the Northeastern U.S. In the church services I ran into a well-known surgeon who had operated on me several years earlier and a company president I knew by reputation. These guys were all smart and I wondered what they knew that I didn't.

Later, I attended a Sunday School class entitled "Christianity 101." It was taught by Pastor Doug Gray, who explained the basics of Christian faith in a simple, dynamic way. At one point, Doug spoke about the gift of blissful eternal life. He stood on a chair and asked, "Do you know what eternity is?" He pointed out a window and said, "It starts somewhere out that window, comes right through here," then he pointed out a window on the other side of the room, "and it goes out that window and keeps on going. Forever." I thought, "What if this is true?" and decided to find out whether it was or not.

Over several years, I explored Christianity and found it was misrepresented by the media and our culture. Once I understood the facts, my opinions changed and faith became credible.

The terms "stumbling stone" and "stumbling block" are used in the Bible and refer to things that misdirect one's thinking and become obstructions, or stumbling stones, to a person's faith.[1] The more I learned, the more I realized that stumbling stones are strewn about widely and in unexpected places.[2] They're insidious, and people are affected by them without even realizing it. Skepticism abounds in movies, television shows, comedy routines, college campuses, and the print media. Often the bias is subtle—spoken in a few words, shown in a facial expression, or communicated in editorial decisions that choose which stories get told and which don't. In this environment it's easy to dismiss Christianity.

Our natural tendency is to fit in with others, and given the skeptical nature of our society, "fitting in" means distrusting and dismissing religion. In order to break out of this comfort zone, something has to happen. In my case, that "something" was Dr. Dave. If he hadn't opened my mind in the beginning, I'd still be trudging on the same old frustrating treadmill without the hope and strength I've found in Christ.

3

Philosophy 101

The Road to Disbelief: A Case Study

  Mittineague Methodist Church was a white middle class church in the white middle class town of West Springfield, Massachusetts, where I grew up during the 50's and 60's. It was a white clapboard building that had stained glass windows, a pipe organ and a steeple with a bell. Going to church was a dignified affair, with the men dressed in suits and the ladies wearing their "Sunday best" dresses. The children were dressed likewise and freshly scrubbed.

  My family had become Methodist by default. When my maternal grandparents looked for a church, West Springfield was a rural farm town and Mittineague was the closest Protestant church. Catholicism wasn't an option for a family with Yankee roots extending back to the Revolutionary War.

  The family owned a 1931 Essex that had no heat, but the car reliably kept the weather out except for the time the goats ate its fabric roof. Winter forced the kids to snuggle together under a blanket, and my grandfather put chains on the tires so they could make it down the poorly plowed dirt road. Going to church could be a project, but they went each week without fail.

The only objection to the church was expressed by my grandfather, Fritz, who was of German descent and worked as a plumber in a local brewery. His problem was that the Methodists, who discourage alcohol use, used grape juice and "not even real wine" for Communion.

My parents, Chet and Ginny, saw to it that I made it to Sunday School almost every week along with my brothers, Jim and Don. We learned about God, Jesus, the meanings of the holidays and John Wesley, the circuit-riding founder of Methodism. American society was exuberant with pride and patriotism. Institutions like churches, the American Legion, fraternal groups, women's auxiliaries, and the Boy Scouts were esteemed; my parents remain proud to this day that all three of their sons became Eagle Scouts.

The United States was fighting a Cold War against the godless communists. We unquestioningly believed in God, and that he was on our side. The U.S. was led by John F. Kennedy, a young, vibrant, personable war hero who reflected the nation's vision of itself.

It was like this until November 22, 1963, when the President was killed and his assassin murdered, leaving the country speculating about who was behind it and why. Soon after, huge cultural changes began to occur. The civil rights movement gained strength and shook "the establishment." Photos of hooded Ku Klux Klansmen gathered around flaming crosses ran in the press. Marchers were fire-hosed, activists murdered, and churches bombed while race riots burned cities. Even in Springfield, across the river from my hometown, the National Guard was called out to protect civil rights marchers. In the midst of this turmoil, the

April 8, 1966 issue of *Time* magazine appeared on newsstands. In large, stark, red letters on a black background, the cover asked "Is God Dead?"

Three months later, Richard Speck committed the first mass murder of the electronic age by murdering eight student nurses in Chicago. The war in Vietnam turned white hot, with thousands of Americans coming home in body bags and the government replacing the dead with draftees. The anti-war movement clamored that our involvement in the war was immoral, and draft resisters fled to Canada. During 1968, Martin Luther King, Jr. and Bobby Kennedy were assassinated, while former Alabama Governor George Wallace ran for president by railing against the "pointy-headed bureaucrats" and the intellectuals he felt were losing the war and ruining the country. Thousands of demonstrators tried to disrupt the Democratic National Convention in Chicago, but were beaten and arrested by police on national television. The nation was angrily polarized, with each side believing to the bone that it was right.

"Sex, Drugs & Rock 'n' Roll" became the slogan of the young, "hippies" dropped out of society, the newly available birth control pill made "free sex" possible, drugs – especially hallucinogenic LSD – became widely used, and hard driving rock 'n' roll songs commented on the war and society's shortcomings. It also promoted substance abuse, both in lyrics and by example. Within three years, three of its superstars — Jimi Hendrix, Janis Joplin and Jim Morrison — were dead because of it.

In June 1969, Senator Ted Kennedy drove his car off a bridge, drowning his female companion. Later that summer, Charles Manson's "family" went on a grisly killing spree that made Richard Speck's murders look like child's play. In a gesture that captured the essence of the times, the killers scrawled the words "helter skelter" on a refrigerator in a victim's blood.

It had been just over three years since *Time* asked "Is God Dead?" and the world was in an accelerating downward spiral. With this backdrop, I went away to college.

I began my college career at Drew University in Madison, NJ. The school was affiliated with the Methodist Church but, for the undergraduates, it was as secular as any other college. The one religious aspect to the campus was a post-graduate seminary that remained aloof from the undergraduate students.

One night, a fellow freshman set up huge speakers in a window facing the seminary. In the early hours of the morning, he engulfed the campus with the first lines of the "The Soft Parade" by The Doors. Lead singer Jim Morrison belted out:

> *"When I was back there in seminary school*
> *there was a person there who put forth the proposition*
> *that you could petition the Lord with prayer*
> *.......petition the Lord with prayer*
> *.......petition the Lord with prayer*
> YOU CANNOT PETITION THE LORD WITH PRAYER!!!!!"[1]

Within a few days I attended my first Philosophy 101 class, which was taught by Dr. John W. Copeland. Dr. Copeland was older, with thinning white hair and a kindly demeanor. The first assignment: write an essay on the question, "Does God Exist?"

The expected answer was "no" and I provided Dr. Copeland with many reasons to be skeptical. I was rewarded with a good grade for this. Regrettably, I truly believed my conclusions and embarked on a life of atheism, proud self-reliance and stress.

My guess is that newly found freedom, combined with an anti-religious and smugly skeptical academic atmosphere, has claimed many victims among college students. Unfortunately, once one leaves college, the popular culture also promotes the anti-religious viewpoint. Unless a person deliberately seeks out religion, it's easy to dismiss it because disbelief is so pervasive.

The popular skepticism about God, along with my own experience in Philosophy 101, created a huge stumbling block for me. My own logic had dismissed God, while my classmates, the popular culture and the undeniable events of the day supported my conclusion. Unbelief was rampant, and I saw no reason to question it.

A variety of influences caused me, an unquestioning churchgoer, to reject religion. Other skeptics will have different stories, but some things will be universal. Our anti-religious culture, the horrors caused by humanity, the random devastation of natural disasters, and the views of peers affect everyone. Bundled together, they seem to create a strong case against God. But once a person is aware of these influences, looks at them skeptically, and objectively learns about Christianity, belief in God and Christ becomes possible.

4

Who Is Jesus?

*People generally agree that Jesus was a "wise man." But it's a huge leap from "wise man" to being the Son of God, and the idea is farfetched.
Why should anyone believe it?*

Most of us know something about Jesus. At Christmas, we hear of his humble birth to a virgin.[1] Easter teaches of Christ's crucifixion,[2] followed by his rising from the dead.[3] In between these events, he raised the dead,[4] healed the sick,[5] walked on water,[6] and fasted for forty days in the desert.[7] How could any reasonable person believe any of this really happened?

The answer is that all of this was possible because he was what he claimed to be: both man and God.[8] Through his godly power he was able to do supernatural things.

We're skeptical of claims like this, and rightfully so. Over the ages, persuasive frauds seeking money, power and influence have drawn unsuspecting people into costly and even fatal schemes. Considering the power claimed for Christ, it would seem easy to dismiss him as just another fake whose exploits were embellished over time. However, there is convincing evidence to support his authenticity.

People disagree over some aspects of Christ's life, but his rationality and intelligence are beyond question. If Jesus was just a smart man, would he have challenged the Jewish hierarchy by claiming to be the Son of God, thereby committing the capital crime of blasphemy and bringing an execution upon himself?[9] His actions make sense only if he really was the Son of God, and the crucifixion was necessary for the fulfillment of his earthly mission.

His disciples confirmed his identity by their behavior. In the night before he was crucified, they tried to vanish into the woodwork and deny their association with him.[10] Days later, after seeing the risen Christ,[11] the disciples committed their lives to spreading the gospel[12] and suffered violent deaths because of it.[13] If they hadn't witnessed the resurrected Christ, why would they have done this?

Another compelling reason to believe in Jesus is his fulfillment of Old Testament prophecies. The Old Testament contains over 300 references[14] to the coming of the Messiah (the anticipated "anointed one" and King of the Jews),[15] all of which were written more than 400 years before the birth of Jesus.[16] The prophecies note specific characteristics of the Messiah. A brief sampling of them includes:

Lineage: Prophecy dictates the Messiah's genealogical line.[17] This requirement eliminates over 99.9% of the Jewish people, but Christ fits it.

Crucifixion: The piercing of his hands and feet is noted in a passage written 800 years before the Romans even used crucifixion.[18] A prophecy that his bones would not be broken also relates to crucifixion. In order to hasten death the victim's legs were typically broken, but Christ died before the time for this arrived and his bones were not broken.[19]

Birth in Bethlehem: He was to be born in this small town with under 1000 residents.[20]

Based on the genealogical requirement alone, fewer than 1/10 of 1% of Jewish men qualify. Of those, how many were born in tiny Bethlehem? How many of these died on the cross without having their legs broken? What about the hundreds of other prophecies that further reduce the field? When the mathematical chances of the prophecies coming true in one individual are calculated, the result is astonishing: less than one in 100,000,000,000,000,000. This is the probability of randomly picking up one particular coin out of silver dollars stacked two feet deep across all of Texas.[21]

As impressive as all this may be, it is not as convincing as the change that happens within believers. When people come to faith, it's common for them to gain an inner peace and an ability to deal with life's challenges with calmness and strength. Christian testimonials are almost too common to be remarkable, except that they express extraordinary improvements in each person's life that were beyond reach before they found Christ.

Convincing evidence attests that Jesus is everything he claimed to be: the Son of God. He is teacher, healer, miracle worker and savior. And he proves this today by continuing to influence the lives of those who come to him.

5

Prayer

What is prayer? Why doesn't it always work? Does it ever work?

✣✣✣✣✣✣✣✣✣✣

"I'm running late. Please don't let this traffic jam tie me up." "This exam is going to be really tough. Please help me pass it." "My sister just got a bad diagnosis. Please help her beat the illness." For many of us, these requests to God are automatic reactions. They can also be the closest we ever get to a relationship with God.

These are called "prayers of petition," in which God is asked to provide a response to the petitioner's request. Sometimes the desired result happens, and sometimes it doesn't. In a random world, it would seem that the same sort of outcomes would occur: sometimes things would work out and sometimes they wouldn't. If we think getting our wishes fulfilled is the only purpose of prayer, it's no surprise that unanswered prayers would cause people to doubt the presence or caring of God.

The question shouldn't be "Why didn't God answer my prayer?" but "How does prayer work?" or "Am I missing the point by focusing on my desires while ignoring the more important attributes of prayer?" An understanding of prayer as designed by God helps explain this.

Prayer is a private conversation between a person and God. Jesus uses the Aramaic word "Abba" for "Father" when praying to God. This translates as "Dad," indicating a personal, intimate and loving relationship.[1] We are invited to pray (talk) to God, who knows everything about you,[2] and offers you the same sort of unconditional love and support that a loving earthly father does.[3] We're encouraged to bring any and all thoughts to God,[4] with the expectation that through examination of the issues and God's guidance, we'll find peace and an appropriate course of action.[5]

Many problems have obvious solutions and are dealt with quickly. Some take a lot of time and prayer to resolve, but in the end they reach a successful conclusion. And then there are those that may never be resolved. In cases like these, God offers strength and comfort. This gives the believer the peace that comes from knowing he has soulfully examined the situation and has acted in accordance with the wishes of God. He's able to put the problem in perspective, knowing that it's a small part of a temporary life on earth that will eventually end in a peaceful, eternal afterlife. And then he can move on without the emotional baggage that weighs so many people down.

To those who don't know God, this can seem like a cop-out[6] that's used as an excuse for walking away from difficult situations. This ignores two facts. First, prayer often does solve problems. Second, there truly are issues that resist solution. The conflicts in the Middle East, the mutual animosity of divorced couples, the pain that comes with the death of a child, and the hurt that's part of broken relationships are all situations that are difficult to resolve, even with the help of God. In these situations, peace with God may be the best outcome possible.[5]

Our emotions can be barriers to prayer. Sometimes they override our determination to work through God and cause us to instinctively and unreflectively chart our own courses. This is usually when we get into trouble and learn lessons the hard way. But when we're through trying to do it on our own and are ready to talk, he's patient and always there waiting for us to come around.[6]

Our society's appetite for psychological advice demonstrates how common the need for support is. It's the reason TV and radio psychologists like Drs. Phil and Laura are so popular, that the self-help departments in book stores are so large, and that psychiatrists, psychologists, and numerous support groups thrive. Unlike the therapy du jour, prayer always offers peace, support, perspective and strength: the strength of God. This can't be found on a radio talk show, Oprah Winfrey's television program or inside a bottle of pills, but it's readily available in the prayerful relationship between a believer and God.[7]

"There is a God-shaped hole in everyone's heart" is a concept I heard during my first months at First Central Baptist Church, but I didn't know what it meant. Eventually, I came to understand that in my attempts to deal with intractable problems, I was scrambling around trying to reconcile irreconcilable differences and fix problems that couldn't be fixed. I was exasperated and frustrated. To make matters worse, I didn't believe in the afterlife, and felt that my life was frittering away in dealing with hassles day after day. This created even more exasperation. For me, the mental space that was constantly abuzz with these issues was my God-shaped hole.

I finally opened my heart to God. Those of us who have children know the total, unconditional love we have for them. This is the kind of love God has for us, and this is what he responds with if we open our hearts to him. If we trust in God, a meaningful relationship with him will develop through prayer and a palpable sense of peace will grow within.

Over time, my prayers gave me insight into dealing with issues and into determining which problems I couldn't solve. This helped me gain an inner peace that had always eluded me. Other people, especially my wife and kids, noticed a change in me, because my infamously bad temper all but disappeared. Other believers have experienced the same thing; it's as though the fight-or-flight mechanism that once kicked in at the slightest provocation had been short-circuited and reserved for use on rare occasions.

We can petition God for particular requests, but whether or not he responds to them in the way we want isn't the point. I wonder what would happen if God actually granted all prayer requests. How could he fulfill the wishes of contradictory prayers? Don't the combatants on both sides of a war usually believe God is on their side and pray to him for victory? Don't thousands of people pray every day to win the lottery? Answering everyone's prayers in the way the petitioners want is obviously impossible.

God has given man free will, and he wants us to use it to come to him. If petitions were always granted, wouldn't everyone become a believer just because they'd know God would act as their servant? Wouldn't this be tantamount to God offering a bribe to entice man to believe in him? The idea that all prayers will be answered in the way sought by the petitioner is clearly unworkable because (1) answering contradictory prayers is impossible, and (2) it would undermine man's free will.

Having written this, I personally know that God responds to prayer when he sees fit. When my older son, Jon, was four years old, my wife Lisa and I were looking for a church to attend. I was an atheist, but felt it was only fair to expose him to organized religion, and let him grow up before I let on what I thought about God.

I thought about this a lot, and wished I could bring myself to believe in God so I could attend church without being hypocritical. In short order, I heard radio talk shows that discussed religious topics I had questions about. The same thing happened with articles in the print media. After having a number of questions answered, I brought the subject up with a respected business associate. This was a real eye-opener since he turned out to be a devout Christian and, since I asked, he was delighted to explain to me what he believed and why. I was intrigued by all of this, but still didn't believe in God. I just thought I was more aware of religious stuff that had always been out there now that I was thinking about it.

Then it happened.

I read to Jon nightly, and every evening for weeks he asked me to read *P. J. Funnybunny*. There were lots of books in his room, including around 50 Golden Books—the thin ones with identical gold and black spines—that were stored together on one shelf. I knew one of those books was *My Little Golden Book About God* which we had never read. As I entered his room, I said my first genuine prayer in decades, and told God that if Jon wanted to read that Golden Book instead of "P.J." I would believe.

Jon had "P.J" in his hands, put it on his bed, walked over to the bookcase, pulled out the "God" book, and handed it to me, saying, "I want to read this tonight." I got shivers up my spine then, and I'm getting them now, writing about this after all these years.

Other situations have occurred in which I believe that God's hand was apparent. In all of these, the common element of my prayers was sincerity of belief and an absence of worldly, self-promoting motives. Maybe that's the key, maybe not. I don't know of anyone who understands the mystery of prayer, and it may not be possible to.

My experience with my son and the book is a personal example of the power and mystery of prayer, but it's no more amazing than the peace prayer offers to all believers. Personal prayer with God is the direct and readily available way to bring his peace and joy into your life.[8] It can, and does, change lives.

6

Forgiveness

We live in a nasty world populated by self-centered, ruthless people. Isn't the Christian obligation to forgive others a weak, impractical response to offenses that puts Christians at the mercy of the merciless?

He had turned 80 and was suffering from kidney failure. His skin was wrinkled and loose-fitting, and his hands trembled weakly. His dry throat made him speak softly, and listeners had to draw near to hear him. He could converse, but sometimes lost track of the subject. Other times, he would sit silently, and you weren't sure whether he heard you. Months of inactivity had left him with no muscle tone; when he was brought to the hospital this time, he had to be lifted out of the car and into a wheelchair.

The soul inhabiting this declining body had been given an interesting ride. He labored in the family business at the age of eight, and as a 6'3" work-hardened young man, had lived a devil-may-care life. This had gotten him into fights, leaving him with a gunshot wound in his arm and glass fragments in his foot from a car accident in which his convertible rolled over and came to rest upside down.

He took up flying in the 1940's. His recklessness led him to clip the tops off the trees at his girlfriend's house, bounce the wheels off the roof of a barn, and fly under telephone wires. At age 26, he married and built his family a brick house on the top of a hill. One fateful day, he buzzed the living room picture window as his wife stood inside, cradling their third child. She was not amused, and in submission to responsibility he hung up his wings.

With his attention fixed on being a provider, his interests changed. He rebuilt a Model T Ford, revamped a bus to create one of the early RV's and took up square dancing. He founded a company that employed fifty and provided the income to build a large house, buy a lakefront cottage, own boats, educate his family, and take them on trips. Always a "people person," he was a successful salesman who had a ready smile and fresh joke for everyone. He had been married for over fifty years to the woman who stood by him now.

My father was a weakened old man reaching the end of his life, and concerned about the hereafter. He was fond of telling about a near-death experience he had while coming out of anesthesia years earlier. His vision was of lush green valleys, cool running streams and total tranquility. He wanted to stay, but an angel appeared and told him that it was not his time. He woke up, and believed that this place was his destiny.

He had said the Lord's Prayer, and prayed for others, nightly for his entire life. In our discussions, he always said he wasn't afraid of death. This was usually followed by an admission that he had done some bad things and regretted them, but had lived a good life. The unspoken message was that he didn't know for sure if he was going to heaven, and the uncertainty weighed on him.

I asked him if he'd feel better if he thought God would see only the good he had done, and not the bad. He agreed that he would. I explained that this is what happens when you admit your sins to God, repent of them, and believe that Jesus died for your sins. By doing this, you're telling God that you understand Christ's sacrifice, accept it, and are grateful for it. This washes away your misdeeds, and you get an express ticket to heaven.

My dad was already two-thirds of the way there: he admitted his sins and repented of them. But believing in Jesus was hard for him. I don't know if he truly accepted Christ or not. If he did, he was forgiven by God, and had a place in heaven he could be sure of even before he got there. God's forgiveness of all of our misdeeds and failings, and the entry into heaven that comes with it, is a keystone of Christianity and the model for the forgiveness Christians give to others.

The ability to forgive is not limited to God; Christians do it every day. It's a tool Christians use in dealing with people who hurt them. There are endless varieties of hurtful behavior: someone makes a derogatory comment to you; a colleague takes credit for your work; a relative spreads false rumors about you that result in strained relations among family members; a gunman robs your store; a drifter murders your child. There are many affronts in life, from the trivial to the tragic. When these situations arise, the victim is in the position of forgiver.

Many people think that Christians must always forgive the offender.

Unconditional forgiveness (automatically forgiving a perpetrator without apology or contrition from them) is, at best, emotionally difficult to give. At worst, it's an invitation to the world to use Christians as doormats who must senselessly forgive all offensive acts. Is unconditional forgiveness expected of Christians, or can they follow a more realistic course of action?

The answer begins with God's method of forgiving us as individuals. In order to receive forgiveness from God, Christians must (1) confess their sins,[1] (2) repent of them[2] (the term "repent" means "to turn away from sin"[3]) and (3) believe that Jesus died to atone for their sins.[4] The first two steps require the offender to examine his actions, admit wrongdoing, and forswear the conduct. The third step is unknowable by humans, so forgiveness by humans is limited to the first two steps.

Forgiveness between people follows God's pattern.[5] Christians must forgive those who sin against them, just as God forgives the sins of repentant believers.[6] But, like God, Christians aren't obligated to forgive unless the offender acknowledges the wrong and commits to changing his behavior. Stripped of religious verbiage, this is what people do when they apologize and have the apology accepted.

The willingness to forgive may seem to be a sign of weakness, but it's really a practical device for salvaging relationships. If a perpetrator tells his victim that he's aware of the destructive act he's committed, asks for forgiveness (apologizes), and then follows through in changing his conduct, two things are likely to happen. First, the victim will be gratified that the offender recognized the problem and was thoughtful enough to address it. Second, the behavior is not repeated. This restores a workable relationship.

In the absence of repentance and forgiveness, the repair of a damaged relationship is impossible. People can still interact with each other, but the underlying trust can't be restored and the old relationship can't be rejuvenated.

Christians can also choose to forgive without contrition from the offender. Forgiving a person under these circumstances brings one closer to God and enhances the peace that God gives. In acting peacefully and without retribution, the forgiver acts in a way that's pleasing to God. Knowing this, the Christian is able to tolerate the offense without holding grudges or focusing on "getting even."[7] In reducing the self-destructive emotions that can make one unhappy, depressed and sick, forgiveness benefits the forgiver even if the offender is unapologetic. This is the benefit of God's peace.

The absence of an apology can show that the relationship is not viable, and enables the Christian to walk away from it in good conscience. Christians are commanded "as far as it depends on you (to) live at peace with everyone."[8] Implicit in this verse is the idea that there are some people you will never be able to get along with, no matter how hard you try. In these cases, the Christian should peacefully back away from the relationship.[9]

Sometimes, people commit the same sins repeatedly and, if they also repeatedly repent, Christians are still to forgive them.[10] A Christian who forgives hurtful behavior is not expected to leave himself unprotected from the same conduct in the future.[11] My grandfather's sage advice, spoken with a heavy Polish accent, was "Fool me once, shame on you. Fool me twice, shame on me." It's prudent advice for Christians, who are not expected to be naïve and vulnerable to the ways of the world.

Forgiveness doesn't exonerate bad conduct, and it doesn't condone avoidance of civil or criminal penalties. Occasionally, the parent of a murder victim will forgive the murderer. This may give the criminal a measure of peace, but it's probably more beneficial to the parent, who can then more readily draw on God's strength. Forgiveness doesn't necessarily mean that the parent doesn't want the killer punished. Forgiven criminals will still be punished, and the penalties can be supported by the forgiver.[12]

Personal forgiveness doesn't grant salvation to the wrongdoer because determination of salvation is God's responsibility. Eternal life with Jesus can be achieved only if the individual believes in Christ, confesses, and repents. Since only God knows the hearts of men, he alone determines whether a person goes to heaven.[13]

Christian forgiveness of others boils down to this:

- *If the offender apologizes and renounces his conduct, the Christian must forgive him. This can repair a damaged relationship.*

- *If the offender doesn't apologize, the Christian may choose to forgive him. The forgiver should protect himself from future offenses and possibly terminate the relationship. Forgiveness dissipates hate, anger and bitterness, and this enables the Christian to peacefully move on.*
- *Forgiving on a personal level doesn't exempt an offender from civil or criminal penalties and has no bearing on whether that person gets into heaven.*
- *The benefits of forgiveness go to the forgiver, not the offender.*

The idea that Christians must unconditionally forgive misdeeds and give offenders a free ride, enabling perpetrators to indiscriminately repeat their behavior, is incorrect. Unfortunately, it's a common misperception that portrays a strength of Christian faith as a weakness.

7

Redemption and Salvation

Somehow Christianity turns hopelessness into joy. Most of us know people who have experienced this, but we don't understand it and sometimes think there's something wrong with the people it's happened to. How is this transformation possible?

After months on a waiting list for a heart-lung transplant, the wife of one of my employees died. She had been a violent and self-destructive person who used drugs and had run-ins with the law. In her last several years she joined a church and became a Christian. The funeral was held in her church, Daniel's New Bethel Church of God in Christ, which was housed in an aging former synagogue in a tough part of town. The sanctuary needed paint and was adorned by a cross that had been placed over the old Star of David behind the lectern. Except for me and one of my employees, all of the attendees were very well-dressed black people.

As the preacher spoke, his points were emphasized by trills from an electronic keyboard at the side of the church. The clear message was "this is not a sad time, it is not a time for tears! This is Sister Betty's homegoing party!" And while the congregants had sympathy for Betty's husband, they were truly happy for Betty. It was the most upbeat funeral I had ever attended. Truth be told, it was the *only* upbeat funeral I had ever attended.

How could this be such a jubilant occasion? After living a decidedly un-Christian lifestyle until just a few years earlier, why was everyone so confident that Betty was in a better place? The answer is redemption and salvation.

Redemption means "purchase."[1] An example of redemption is when God punished Egypt by striking down every firstborn throughout the nation.[2] The enslaved Hebrews were instructed by God to sacrifice lambs and put the blood on their doorframes.[3] God then passed over the marked houses and spared the occupants from death.[4] This event is celebrated by the Jewish holiday called Passover.[5] The lives of the Hebrew firstborn were redeemed, or purchased, from God by the sacrifice of the lambs.

According to the Bible, sin is displeasing to God and causes separation from him.[6] As imperfect beings, men commit sins and by doing so separate themselves from God. In order to regain good standing with God, man must pay a price to have his sins taken away.[7]

This is not as abstract an idea as it may appear. As children, we've all done something that caused a parent to be angry. When the parent is angry, communication is difficult and parental support seems to have evaporated. This can cause intense feelings on the part of the child, since the parent has control over food, clothing, shelter and emotional support. In order to rectify the situation, a price has to be paid. The price is generally in terms of pride, which is sacrificed in issuing an apology.

When a person commits a sin, it's known by at least two entities: the sinner and God.[8] This creates a barrier, similar to that between a disobedient child and his parent, that a believer knows is between himself and God. Just as the child restores his good standing with his parent by apologizing to him, a believer renews his relationship with God by confessing his sin and repenting his conduct.

The redemption from sin is a concept that goes back thousands of years. Pagans made sacrifices of bulls, rams,[9] sheep[10] and even their sons and daughters[11] to gods to gain their favor. For many years after Moses, Jews continued to offer sacrifices to pagan gods in defiance of the one true God.[12] Even the God of the Hebrews (the same God worshipped by Christians) commanded specific sacrifices for the Jews to carry out in atonement for their sins.[13] These included bulls,[14] goats,[15] doves, pigeons[16] and lambs which were to be "without defect" and ritually slaughtered. Upon completion of the sacrifice and the confession of the sinner, the sins were forgiven.[17]

Jesus is called the "Lamb of God." This is because he was the ultimate sacrifice that redeemed (purchased)—and continues to redeem—mankind.[18] Christ was the only perfect (i.e. "without defect") human ever to have lived, since he was the only one who totally lived by the impossibly high standards he taught. With the sacrifice of Jesus, no other sacrifices are needed; his is sufficient to cover the sins of all men at all times. Man now only needs to believe in Jesus, confess his sins, and repent in order to be forgiven and seen as clean and sinless by God.[19]

Salvation, or being "saved" means that the believer has had his sins forgiven by God and will spend eternity with him.[20] In order to receive salvation, a person must accept Christ as his lord and savior. This means he must truly believe that Jesus is the Son of God, and that his teachings are those of God. By doing this, the believer acknowledges that he understands the sacrifice of Christ and gratefully accepts it through the grace of God. Christ redeems the person from sin and, being washed clean, the believer is qualified for salvation and will spend eternity in heaven.

Heaven isn't fully described in the Bible, but we have clues as to what it's like. The Lord's Prayer, taught by Jesus, includes the line "…your will be done on earth as it is in heaven."[21] Christ came to earth to teach mankind God's will, and it's summed up in the Golden Rule: "…in everything do unto others what you would have them do unto you."[22] Since God's will is done in heaven, it's a place where every soul operates according to this rule. It must be a wonderful, peaceful place.

Life is a mixed bag of triumphs, failures, love, hate, honesty, duplicity and every other set of contradictory behaviors and emotions. Sometimes we inflict our flaws on the world and sometimes, probably mostly, the world inflicts its flaws on us. Some people are able to cope with this life and even thrive in it. Others, like Sister Betty, are swallowed up by life's difficulties and wander through it devoid of hope unless they find Christ.

The Christian promise of salvation knows no boundaries. No matter who we are, Jesus loves us and gave his life so we could be forgiven and spend eternal life in heaven, a place that extinguishes the hurt of earthly life and replaces it with bliss.

This was the focus of the funeral service that day at Daniel's New Bethel Church of God in Christ. It's the reason Sister Betty's passing away was the most joyous event in her life.

8

Satan

In "The Exorcist" the main character is taken over by Satan and made evil. "Rosemary's Baby" is fathered by Satan and looks part human/part animal. Do Christians believe these portrayals are real?

    The 726 Bus from the train station dropped us off. The stop was in a pleasant neighborhood with well kept apartment buildings, a park and a bike trail. Children happily played outside despite the cold temperature and the dreariness of the day. I was surprised because I thought my destination would be in a remote, isolated area.
    After walking a few hundred feet down a gravel path that ran alongside a fast-moving stream, the entrance appeared. I had seen pictures of this gate over the years and had the impression it was large and imposing, but it wasn't. It was in a passageway through a two-story stucco building with a tile roof, and it was only about three feet wide and a little over six feet high.
    Written in wrought iron in the top of the gate were the words "Arbeit Macht Frei": "Freedom Through Work." This was the entrance to the Dachau Concentration Camp, the first facility of its kind in Nazi Germany and the model for those that followed.

The camp's original purpose was to intern those whom the government determined were politically dangerous and to deter other dissidents. It also supplied slave workers for quarries, road construction and armament production. Many of the undernourished, minimally clothed and overworked prisoners labored in unsafe conditions and fell victim to "annihilation through work." Others died from hunger, disease, exposure or all three. Suicide was common.

A number of prisoners also died from medical experiments. Many were purposely infected with malaria, tuberculosis and other diseases. Some were subjected to rapid pressure loss in a decompression chamber to simulate the conditions faced by pilots who bailed out at high altitude. Others were placed in ice baths for hours to evaluate re-warming methods. There were also experiments to test ways to stop bleeding.

A tour of the camp underscored its brutality. The roll call area is a huge open yard where thousands of poorly clothed prisoners stood for at least an hour daily in all weather. In the Bunker, victims were kept in dark isolation for up to three months and in two foot square cells for up to three days. They were strapped to "flogging blocks" for whipping and subjected to "tree hanging" in which the prisoner's hands were bound behind his back and his body suspended by his wrists for hours.

Then there is the firing range, with the "blood pit," where mass executions took place. And finally, the extermination facility which consisted of four connected rooms: the first where up to 150 victims were to remove their clothing, the next where "showers" discharged lethal gas, then the storage room for the corpses and, last, the crematorium.[1]

This place can only be described as evil. And while it's notable for its scale, the depth of its depravity and the systematization of its processes, the human malevolence it reveals is all too common. Charles Manson......Ted Bundy......terrorist bombings...... violent home invasion......child abuse......executive fraud...... the list goes on and on.

Evil is real. Satan is the personification of this reality.

Evil is that which is morally bad, wrong, wicked, malevolent, harmful, injurious, corruptive or destructive.[2] Jesus is the teacher of love; Satan is called the "tempter"[3] and is on the opposite side, enticing men to evil conduct.

Christians disagree about whether Satan is a literal entity or a symbolic one. If Satan is an actual being who draws individuals into sinful behavior,[4] then the conflict between good and evil is simply explained and understood. If the devil is a literary device employed to make man aware of an ongoing personal struggle within himself because of his own nature,[5] the concept is more complex but the effect is the same. We understand there's a selfish, immoral component of our being that fights against moral behavior.

In this discussion, the disparity will be regarded as a distinction without a difference and the term "Satan" will be used interchangeably to mean both the literal being and the part of our personalities that drives us toward harmful conduct. In both cases, the Christian is aware of the forces pulling at him, and this awareness is a significant step to leading a Christian life.

All of us have weaknesses that provide Satan with opportunities to work. Some have short tempers that can lead to cursing at your children, episodes of road rage, or homicide in the heat of the moment. Addictions perpetuate a violent drug trade that kills bystanders while the user himself is devastated by a loss of jobs, relationships, self-respect and sometimes life itself. Others are predisposed to marital infidelity that causes mistrust, divorce and, in cases where children are involved, broken homes that leave innocent children with emotional scars. When situations that test our weaknesses arise, Satan is always there to intensify the urge to do the damaging thing.

The Bible offers practical advice in dealing with these conflicts. In the above examples, for instance, a person avoids the negative consequences of his behavior if he heeds warnings against fits of rage, intoxication[6] and adultery.[7] Behaving biblically not only avoids trouble, it has another positive effect: the believer's place in heaven is enhanced because he has striven to live according to God's rules.[8]

This leads to the question of hell. While people freely talk about heaven, the departed loved ones they believe are there, and their personal concept of what heaven is like, it's unfashionable to discuss hell. The politically correct crowd seems determined to excuse even the most socially destructive behavior in paying homage to what they apparently believe is the ultimate moral state: non-judgmentalism.[9] In this mindset, there is no objective definition of right or wrong, and hell is an antiquated and absurd notion.[10] This view is no doubt comforting for those who "do it if it feels good" and put personal gratification above all else. But the evaporation of moral standards it promotes doesn't make sense if we're to have a cohesive and successful society.

For Christians, the rules of behavior are spelled out in the Bible. Conduct that violates them is unacceptable and has consequences. These consequences can include hell, which is as much a reality as heaven.[11] God determines whether a person is saved and will enter heaven or be relegated to hell.[12]

If only heaven (and not hell) existed, then no judgment would be rendered to those who violated God's laws by, for example, exterminating millions of people. Having monsters like Hitler or John Wayne Gacy get off with no afterlife at all would be easy for them, and probably just what they expected. Christians are to refrain from seeking revenge themselves, but one of God's roles is to avenge evil.[13] Hell is where this takes place.

There is scant description of hell in the Bible, but authors and artists have tried to define it. In The Inferno, Dante Alighieri wrote of a journey through a hell made up of Nine Circles. These descend into gradually more horrific punishments as the misdeeds of the sinners become greater.[14] Renowned 16th century painters Hieronymus Bosch and Pieter Bruegel painted surreal visions of hell showing fearsome demons imposing diabolical punishments on sinners.[15] These works created the conventional vision of hell for centuries. Today, their fantasies may be part of the reason hell isn't taken seriously.

Various concepts of hell have been expressed over the years. Pope John Paul II stated that "rather than a place, hell indicates the state of those who freely and definitively separate themselves from God" and "exclude themselves from the book of life."[16] Others believe it truly is a "place of literal fire and agony."[17] Some contemporary scholars "contend that those who ultimately reject God will simply be put out of existence in the "consuming fire" of hell"[18] or that it's a state of "self-isolation" so severe that you have "no relationships at all."[19]

The Bible doesn't definitively describe the devil's physical appearance, and the popular images of Satan aren't Christian. He's sometimes depicted as having horns and a goat's hindquarters, as a sharp featured, goateed man with a tail and pitchfork, or as "Sparky," the mascot for the Arizona State University "Sun Devils." These portrayals, which imitate pagan figures like the Greek god Pan, were used to personify evil in medieval times.[20] They've stayed with us, and imaginative new visions of Satan occasionally crop up today. These characters have little to do with biblical teaching, and are probably a hindrance to faith if people believe that Satan's depictions in popular books, movies and television represent Christian belief.

No matter how much our perceptions of heaven and hell change, the Bible remains unchanging. Its moral standards can't be violated with impunity because there are consequences, both in this life and afterward. The secular price we pay for a lack of morality is a lessening of dignity, self respect and trust, as well as in addictions, damaged relationships and crime. After death the price is paid with personal reprobation.

With the stakes this high, the importance of Christ is evident. If we believe in him, our sins are removed and we're saved.[21] We all have personal weaknesses and engage in conduct that should be damning. But Christ's sacrifice turns it around and creates salvation where hell is deserved.

Every human being knows Satan and understands he's always there to nudge us in the destructive direction. Those who know Christ understand the difficulty of the struggle and are aware of the ultimate stakes. But Christians also know that Satan can be defied, both in this life and the next.

9

Sin

What is sin and why is it important?

✣✣✣✣✣✣✣✣✣✣✣

Sin was always a fuzzy concept for me. It brought to mind the preacher in "Inherit the Wind" raging over his daughter's proposed marriage to an evolutionist, Roman Catholic friends going to weekly confession in the 1960's and being assigned recitations of "Hail Marys" in atonement for their sins, and fiery visions of the ultimate penalty for sin, hell.

Sins seemed to come in all sizes, shapes, colors and levels of severity. There were things some Christians felt were sinful, while others didn't. Eating meat on Friday, dancing, drinking alcohol and the use of birth control were a few of these. The only thing that was clear was that whatever sinning you did, if you did enough of it, or did one spectacularly bad thing, you would end up in hell. And hell was a very bad place.

The differences of opinion create confusion about what sin really is, but its definition is simple. It is that which is unacceptable to God.[1] How do we know what is unacceptable to God? The Bible is the rule book.

"Sin" was originally an archery term denoting the distance by which a shot missed the bull's eye. The goal of Christians is to act in ways that are acceptable to God; conduct that's unacceptable to God "misses the mark" and is a sin. As in archery, sins can be minor and miss perfection by little, or they can be huge and miss the whole target.[2]

The idea of sin seems outdated and irrelevant today. In today's society, many of the Bible's rules are ignored, if not ridiculed. This is unfortunate, because the concept of sin is one of the ways God teaches man how to live in a mutually supportive, civil and personally fulfilling way.

The Bible enumerates a number of sins. Six of the Ten Commandments dictate secular behavior like honoring parents, not murdering, not stealing, not committing adultery, not falsely testifying and not coveting your neighbor's wife or possessions.[3] In the New Testament, sinful acts include sexual immorality, hatred, discord, jealousy, envy and drunkenness.[4] Instead, Christians are to practice "love, joy, peace, patience, kindness, goodness, faithfulness, gentleness and self-control."[5]

Nowhere in the New Testament is violence, hate, persecution or retribution condoned. The Christian mindset is summed up in a single command: "Love your neighbor as yourself."[6] Acts that violate this concept are sinful (i.e., they are unacceptable to God). Can anyone disagree that the world would be a better place if we all lived by this ideal? The concept of sin, in teaching man what behaviors to avoid and providing directions for proactive, positive conduct, offers us ways to successfully live together that are deeper than governmental laws.

Human behavior is affected by our individual consciences. This is where the concepts of right and wrong are put into practice.

With some the conscience withers and leaves people with no moral compass. With others, it develops through influences like the culture at large, family, peers, education and religion. People who have no biblical guidance are left with a grab-bag of random factors that vary dramatically from person to person. In the worst case, this produces the antisocial barbarians who belong to violent gangs and whose behavior is ruled by a code of ethics concocted by their peers.

To be sure, many non-Christians have sensible moral standards, and many of these are even codified in law. A certain level of civil behavior is necessary in all cultures just to enable societies to function. Laws against murder, stealing, and running red lights exist for this reason. But these laws tell citizens what they *can't* do in order to protect us from each other. They don't tell us what we *should* do in order to live in a positive and successful way.

In comparison, Christians live according to God's rules, and these go beyond civil and cultural requirements. As a Christian learns more about the Bible, his conscience becomes progressively developed, and it becomes an increasingly important guide. The internalized sense of biblical rightness and wrongness is partly what is meant when a believer says that the Holy Spirit is in him. This is a wonderful thing: while civil laws are restricted to limiting harmful acts, the Bible instructs believers to go further and develop positive qualities like kindness, joy and love and to live responsibly.[7]

The conscience is affected by the spiritual education one receives and this instruction isn't uniform among Christian churches. Understandably, these differences can cause confusion. Some Christian churches profess that certain behaviors are sinful, even though they're not specifically addressed in the Bible. A good example of this is gambling. Roman Catholic churches raise money from Bingo nights and sponsor trips to casinos, but fundamentalist churches frown on it. There are several reasons for the fundamentalist view. One is that there is a possibility of addiction, which would make the behavior sinful when it superceded a person's dedication to God. Addictions can also lead to stealing or lying, which are specifically sinful. Additionally, the Bible says that man should earn his keep, and money obtained through chance would seem to violate this. On the other hand, Roman Catholics rightfully point out that the Bible enjoins a number of behaviors, but gambling isn't one of them. One can argue either side of issues like this, but each side would agree that these areas of disagreement aren't central to faith, and they don't determine whether a person is a Christian or not.

The Christian approach to sin and sinners is expressed in the phrase "hate the sin but love the sinner." This may sound contradictory, but it isn't. The primary feature of Christianity is love, and it's best exemplified by the unconditional love of parents for their child regardless of his actions.

One night when I was in college, I went out carousing. Afterward, I followed a friend home, he in his car and me in mine. As I followed behind, his speeding car hit a heaved patch of asphalt, hopped off the street, and knocked down a telephone pole. I found him bloody and unconscious with his head partially poking out the broken passenger side window. He seemed to be snoring, but the gurgling sound was made as he exhaled through the blood. The door was jammed shut, the engine was on fire, and I couldn't pull him out the window by myself. Luckily, a cop was nearby and the two of us managed to drag him free shortly before the car was engulfed in flames. He lived, suffering "only" a fractured jaw and other less serious injuries.

I knew his parents, and although I dreaded it, I called to tell them what happened. There was no anger, toward either me or their son. There was just overwhelming relief that he was going to be OK.

Did his parents hate his reckless behavior? Yes. Did they hope that his conduct would change? Yes. Did they refuse to accept and love him because of it? Of course not; they loved him as fully as always. Having almost lost him, they may have even loved him more. This is the love that enables us to hate the sin but love the sinner.

This characterizes Christians when they're confronted by unacceptable conduct.

The Bible requires that sinners be treated in the spirit of reconciliation and love.[8] And Christians are specifically told they have "no excuse" for judging others because they, too, are sinners.[9]

People do things that disappoint themselves and God, and they often do the same things repeatedly. St. Paul, an admitted hopeless sinner who was on an expedition to persecute Christians when he was converted by Jesus[10] became a righteous man who dedicated his life to spreading the gospel across the ancient world. His writings of advice and encouragement to far flung churches comprise a significant part of the New Testament. Paul's rock solid faith caused him to be chained,[11] jailed, flogged,[12] beaten with rods, stoned, and shipwrecked three times.[13] But even he was frustrated by his incessant struggle against sin, leading him to write "what I do is not the good I want to do; no, the evil I do not want to do – this I keep on doing."[14] Like Paul, all of us sin, and none of us is in a position to judge others.

Paul's frustration with his sin applies to everyone. Sin prevents us from living as God wishes, but it's hard to avoid it because everyone is tempted by his own desires.[15] Try living in selflessness,[16] generosity toward your enemies,[17] and patience for a day and see how far you get.

Sin is a yardstick we use to measure our lives. Seen in this way, it's much more than something that causes an angry God to condemn the sinner. It tells us when we've acted against the wishes of God and are in need of forgiveness. Forgiveness by God relieves the believer from accumulated feelings of remorse, inadequacy, and guilt. And it reliably provides practical guideposts for living effectively.

10

Judgment Day

Christ saved the soul of one of the criminals he was crucified with shortly before they both died, telling him "today you will be with me in paradise."¹ The idea that a person can lead an evil life but be allowed into heaven at the last minute is not fair and makes no sense.

On June 13, 1983, a twenty-three year old drug addict and prostitute named Karla Faye Tucker was busy. She broke into her ex-lover's apartment with the intention of stealing motorcycle parts. Unexpectedly finding him home in bed, she struck him with a three-foot pickax more than twenty times before turning the weapon on his girlfriend, killing them both. At her trial, Karla Faye proudly recounted the crime, and boasted about the satisfaction she experienced each time she plunged the ax into her victims. If any crime warranted the death penalty, this was it, and it was imposed.

Fast forward to 1998. Karla Faye has spent 14 years in prison and compiled an exemplary record while rehabilitating herself. She converted to Christianity, married a prison chaplain, and now recounted her crime as "the most horrible nightmare of my life." When she was interviewed on national television, her girl-next-door attractiveness, calm demeanor, intelligence and faith supported the notion that this wasn't the same person who committed the crime, but was a new being who deserved to have her sentence reduced. In a campaign to pardon her from the death penalty, many organizations and individuals supported her, including the homicide detective who recommended the death penalty at her trial and some of the victims' siblings. They did not prevail.[2]

At 6:45 AM on February 3rd 1998 a lethal injection was administered. Karla Faye Tucker coughed, let out a soft groan, fell silent and died. Her conciliatory last words included "I'm going to be face-to-face with Jesus now."[3]

Tucker's story raises several issues. One is the legal aspect. Karla may have genuinely become a new person who would be an asset to society: Christian faith has a way of doing that. But coming to faith, and even receiving the forgiveness of the victims, doesn't undo crimes. Belief in Christ will bring God's forgiveness and entry into heaven regardless of the offense,[4] but it doesn't exempt anyone from paying the criminal penalties for crimes.[5] As a practical matter, only God knows what is in the hearts of men, and he will judge accordingly at the proper time.[6] But societies can't wait for God's eternal judgment and must function with enforceable laws.

The idea that people could be hopeless sinners right up to the end of life, find God at the eleventh hour, and then be allowed into heaven was a stumbling stone for me. Why should a person who lives a selfish and abhorrent life be granted the same eternity as those who have tried to live according to the teachings of Jesus? If man isn't held accountable for his actions, what sort of guidance for living does this concept provide? I found the absence of consequences to be unfair and troubling.

The answer to this is on two levels. First, the focus of God is to bring imperfect humans to him. If God were to draw a line in the sand that denied man salvation when he crossed over it (a crime like Karla's would certainly qualify) then that person would have no incentive to change or come to Christ. This would be detrimental to both the sinner—who would live out his life without hope of salvation—and society at large, which would continue to be victimized by offenders who would have nothing to gain by accepting faith and living by Christian ideals.

Second, judgment day is more complex than most people think. The promise of Christianity is that believers will enter heaven to live with Jesus for eternity. A person's deeds during life play no role in whether he gets in or not, since God's grace- given to those who believe in Jesus- provides the admission ticket.[7]

In addition to the judgment that enables the faithful to enter heaven, Jesus conducts another judgment. At this point, believers are judged based on what they've done in life, whether good or bad. The Bible indicates that there are various levels of reward in heaven and an individual's status is determined at this time.[8, 9]

This brings us back to Karla Faye Tucker. Her apparent sincere belief worked to make her final years peaceful and forward looking, despite being on death row. It also gained her eternal life and the opportunity to be "face to face with Jesus." When she saw him, she undoubtedly found him to be not only kind and loving but also the judge who weighed her worldly works. Karla Faye is no doubt in heaven—which is a good place—but in a station appropriate to her deeds.

The concept that our status in the afterlife is influenced by our worldly acts lends gravity to the choices we make and adds meaning to the way we live. It satisfies our sense of justice, and provides a concrete reason for leading a Christian life.

11

The Trinity

The Greeks and the Romans had a number of gods who were responsible for particular aspects of life and the universe. Jews and Muslims have one God who is responsible for everything. But Christians believe in something more complicated and difficult to understand. What is it, and why is it?

Christians believe in the "Trinity."

This can be a confusing concept. It's the term for a "godhead," or divine entity, that is made up of three persons: God the Father, his only son Jesus Christ, and the Holy Spirit. These three parts interact with each other to form the Triune, or three-in-one God. Each is a different manifestation of the one God.[1]

The godhead is one entity, but it appears in different ways. Water is an illustration that helps visualize this. At 32 degrees F it's a solid. If it gets any warmer, it becomes a liquid, and if its temperature rises to 212 degrees F, it becomes airborne as water vapor. In each case it's still water, but it has taken on dramatically different characteristics.

Like water, each of the three parts of the Trinity is wholly God, but each has different duties. Rather than complicating things, the concept of the Trinity simplifies our understanding of the functions of God by separating them into clearly defined parts. Instead of having one mysterious, amorphous, unseeable and unapproachable God who is responsible for everything, we have the following:

- *God the Father, who has created everything. This is the majestic, fearsome God of the Old Testament.*[2]
- *Jesus, the only son of God the Father, who is both God and human.*[3] *As God, he possesses supernatural powers*[4] *and is able to live a perfect life (that is, a life without sin).*[5] *At the same time, his humanity enables him to feel pain,*[6] *joy,*[7] *and anger.*[8] *He was in a man's body and approachable by man. In this form, men could listen to, speak to, and see God in a way not possible before or since. One of the great things about Christ is that, through him, we can relate to God more easily, because when he was on earth he was like us, at least in form. The result is that we can comprehend God more easily because we can put a face on him. This ability to put a kind, familiar face on God—and Jesus is God—helps Christians live in peace instead of in fear of an unseen and incomprehensible deity. This intimate closeness to God was no doubt intended when Jesus came to earth. Transcending all of this is Christ's role as the sacrifice that redeemed sin and granted of salvation to all who believe in him.*
- *The Holy Spirit does the work of God. He hovered over the waters during creation,*[9] *gave Samson power*[10] *and imbued Saul with the gift of prophecy.*[11]

More importantly, the Spirit resides in each of us[12] and works with our individual consciences.[13]

In breaking down God into the Trinity, his complex nature becomes more understandable to man. We know how he wants us to live, because we learned the rules directly from him in the form of Jesus. And we've been given the tools to live according to his teachings through the constant presence of the Holy Spirit.

12

Why Do Bad Things Happen?

Look around. Hatred, confusion, crime, disease, starvation, war, terrorism, earthquakes, floods, fires... the list is endless. Christians believe there is an all-powerful creator who sees all and is active today. And they tell me he's good?

✣✣✣✣✣✣✣✣✣✣

  I ran into a childhood friend at a picnic. His five-year-old nephew had recently died from a heart condition, and I expressed my condolences. But when I brought up prayer, his demeanor changed and he coolly stated, "There is no God." He meant it, and it was difficult to disagree with him.
  Why do these things happen? Why do children suffer and die from cancer? Why does a bus plummet off a mountain road in South America, killing all on board? How about victims of hurricanes, tornadoes or tsunamis? What about war with its casualties? The world is full of diseases, personal tragedies, armed conflicts, and natural disasters that indiscriminately take lives and maim survivors. How can Christians see all this and still believe in a "good" God?

Many people believe that God directs and controls everything. If this were the case, it would be impossible to regard him as good, since he would be the deliberate cause of all these tragedies. But maybe this concept of God is incorrect and he doesn't control everything.[1] If this is the case, then how is the world designed and why?

God created a universe with natural forces that follow their own rules.[2] Man's job is to learn to deal with nature for his own safety and good without the constant intervention of God.[3] Many natural processes work to man's benefit: rain falls, seeds germinate, plants grow and man has food. We've enhanced this by developing more effective agricultural methods. By using natural forces, man produces food, harnesses electricity, fights disease and walks on the moon.

Other forces are highly destructive but are as natural as the beneficial ones. Diseases are caused by viruses or genetic predisposition. Earthquakes are caused by stresses between the tectonic plates. A bus in the Andes Mountains is sent plummeting off a cliff because a tire blows out at a bad time. All of these occur as a result of forces that are part of creation, subject to the rules of nature, and understandable by man.

God has commanded man to subdue the earth. In other words, man is to learn about natural processes, control them and use them for mankind's benefit. As we gain knowledge, problems that have vexed mankind are solved. Diseases have been conquered, earthquake-proof buildings have been built, and food production techniques have been developed to the point where the planet can produce enough food to feed everyone.

But producing enough food is one thing; distributing it is another. Starvation could be eliminated if the authorities in stricken areas would allow food to be brought in. But greed, ethnic hatred, and territoriality conspire to keep this from happening. This goes on because God chooses to give men the ability to make their own choices, and in doing so he must refrain from controlling everything himself. Free will is what makes evil possible.

Then why doesn't God abolish free will? It's because he wants man to love him[4] and the only love that's meaningful is love that's freely given. In order to sincerely love God, man must have the option of either loving God or choosing not to love him. Paradoxically, the free will that enables evil also enables genuine love.[5]

Look at it this way. In totalitarian societies, the leaders often claim to be loved by their people, and the people usually outwardly show affection and loyalty. But it would be foolish to believe that the threat of incarceration, torture or death for those who openly disagree doesn't cause many to falsely declare their love for the dictator. This fake, coerced love isn't genuine and isn't what God wants. The love God desires must be offered voluntarily, without coercion.

Bribery can also be used to elicit sham love. If God actively controlled everything and answered everyone's prayers, wouldn't man automatically "love" him in order to keep the favors coming? The result would be "love" bought and paid for by God.

In 1994, a young exotic dancer named Anna Nichole Smith married J. Howard Marshall, an 89-year-old billionaire, at a Houston drive-through chapel. After showering his bride with millions of dollars in cash and gifts, he died less than a year later. Although Marshall's will left Smith nothing, she claimed that "he always said I could have half," and sued the estate. As the court battle proceeded, there were those who questioned the sincerity of Ms. Smith's love for her late husband.[6] It's this sort of adulterated "love" that God doesn't desire and will not promote.

Man's freedom to make his own decisions gives God affirmation that believers truly love him, but the negative consequence is that others have the license to behave badly. This behavior, which is unacceptable to God but made possible by him, results in all sorts of wrongs.

Those who break God's rules are often powerful, successful, wealthy, influential and esteemed by a world in which fairness and morality mean little. Our culture lionizes people who engage in substance abuse, sexual infidelity, and insatiable greed, while those who criticize them are considered intolerant and out of touch.

It often seems that the world's ethics are fluid, with standards that have no basis other than the personal inclinations of the individuals making them up. The biblical morality that has held our civilization together for thousands of years is given little, if any, consideration. Because of their trust in biblical truths, Christians have historically been persecuted and continue to be in a surprisingly large portion of the world.[7]

God's goodness isn't reflected in the ways of the world, but in the standards he established for human conduct, the strength he offers through prayer, the sacrifice of his son to pay for our sins, and the promise of peace to those who believe. The hope of eternal life puts our earthly trials into perspective and makes living in a Christian way meaningful. He is good because he offers to have a personal relationship with each of us and helps us along the path leading to an afterlife with him. It can be difficult to love God in this world, but the rewards of internal peace and eternal life are worth it.

In the absence of a good God, what hope is there? The secular view was expressed well by the actor Robert DeNiro. Asked whether he believed in God, he replied, "Well, if there is a God he sure has a lot of explaining to do."[8] In other words, God —not man—is responsible for all that has gone on in the world, and it's up to God to justify himself to a Hollywood actor.

The viewpoint so wittily expressed by DeNiro is depressing. There are only two possibilities. First, there is a God, he's not good, and he's not on the side of mankind. He obviously can't be expected to give anyone support in this life, and one can only guess what, if anything, lies in store for us after death. Second, there is no God, the trials we go through are utterly meaningless, and our existence ends when we die.

Given the alternatives, it's no wonder belief in Jesus is so uplifting.

Bad things happen because God has created a world that has its own natural dynamics and is populated by imperfect, independent and self-centered humans. God doesn't always use his power to influence events, but presents the world as a stage upon which man is free to make right or wrong decisions.

Man can decide to come to faith or not. He can choose to try to live by God's standards or not. These decisions, made in a challenging, random, unfair and sometimes tragic world, determine whether a person enjoys the support of God and has the promise of a blissful eternity.

13

War

Conflicts arise and supposedly peace-loving Christians participate in them. Isn't this hypocritical?

In December of 1914, German and Allied soldiers endured insufferable conditions. The trenches they lived in were wet, muddy, cold and often littered with the decaying bodies of their comrades. Rats, lice, nits and the diseases they wrought were constant companions, and medical care was as poor as death was common. The armies would attack each other across "no-man's land," a barren area between the opposing trenches cluttered with shell craters, wrecked equipment and barbed wire. In hand-to-hand combat, the sides bitterly traded the same property back and forth, with no lasting changes. When they weren't fighting in no man's land they were holed up in the trenches where the enemy would shell them with long range artillery. It was terrifying and the soldiers on both sides lived in relentless fear.

Then Christmas Eve arrived. At about 7:30 PM, candles were set on the parapets of the German trenches, and they began to sing. Soon, the British also sang and, between songs, the enemies shouted across to each other. In acts of mutual trust, men from each side climbed out of the trenches and met each other peacefully in no-man's land. Hours later, on Christmas Day, hundreds of soldiers from both sides met to exchange greetings, food, cigarettes and addresses. Some played soccer together.

The day after Christmas, a captain in the Royal Welsh Fusiliers stood above his trench and fired his weapon into the air. His German counterpart also climbed out. They bowed to each other, saluted, and went back down. The German fired his rifle twice into the air, and the war resumed.[1]

The "Christmas Truce" illustrates the Christian dilemma with war. Jesus taught that love of fellow man is our highest aspiration, but our survival sometimes makes violence and war necessary. How can we reconcile this?

The Christian attitude is expressed in the New Testament in verses such as "Love your enemies and pray for those who persecute you,"[2] "If your enemy is hungry, feed him; if he is thirsty give him drink,"[3] "The weapons we fight with are not the weapons of this world,"[4] "Love your neighbor as yourself,"[5] and "Do not take revenge."[6]

Of Christ's own actions the Bible states "...he did not retaliate; when he suffered he made no threats."[7] When Jesus was arrested, a follower drew his sword and cut off the ear of the servant of one of his oppressors. Christ's reaction was to heal the wounded man and order the weapon to be put away.[8] It was during this incident that he warned, "All who draw the sword will die by the sword."[9] Additionally, the commandment "Thou shalt not kill"[10] precludes God's condoning war.

The biblical references above seem to sum up the Christian view of violence and war: that passivity and pacifism are always called for. Claiming to be a follower of Christ while conducting war would be hypocritical.

If this were the case, how could Christians survive in a world among people who don't share Christian ideas of morality, and may even have values that promote aggressiveness? Doesn't this leave Christians defenseless against predators? Aren't Christian ideals of non-reprisal a recipe for subjugation by aggressors?

In fact, there are conditions that allow Christians to engage in military action while remaining loyal to their faith. In Paul's Letter to the Romans, Christians are commanded to "submit to the governing authorities"[11].... (The ruler) does not bear the sword for nothing. He is God's servant, an agent of wrath to bring punishment on the wrongdoer.[12] Later in the New Testament, Christians are urged to "(pray) for kings and all those in authority, that we may live peaceful and quiet lives in all godliness and holiness."[13] It's left to the civil authorities to determine what measures must be taken to ensure that peace is maintained and, if they determine war is necessary, Christians are to submit to their decisions.

There are other points to consider. The first regards the Bible's stance toward war and the people who fight them. In the Book of Ecclesiastes, Solomon lists over a dozen life cycles including birth/dying, planting/uprooting, weeping/laughing and silence/speaking. The final verse is "...a time for war and a time for peace,"[14] expressing the notion that wars—like the other cycles—are inevitable. Jesus himself said, "When you hear of wars and rumors of wars do not be alarmed. Such things must happen."[15]

Jesus's conduct with military men demonstrates his acceptance of them and their occupations. When a Roman officer asks him to cure his ailing servant, Jesus heals the man and then, rather than criticizing the centurion for his occupation, remarks that the officer has faith greater than that found even in Israel.[16] A similar, but even more striking example, occurs when God brings together a "righteous and God-fearing" centurion named Cornelius with the disciple Peter. Peter issues no rebuke to the officer regarding his profession, but instead states that Cornelius has "received the Holy Spirit." Peter then orders "that (Cornelius) be baptized in the name of Jesus Christ," thereby acknowledging to the other Christians in attendance that Cornelius had "received the Holy Spirit just as we have." He also states that God "accepts men who fear him and do what is right."[17] He never suggests the centurion's military occupation was an obstacle to his becoming a Christian.

Christ never denigrated the military or called for its dismantling. On the contrary, he recognized that armed conflicts would be a continuing plague and that the military was necessary to deal with them.

The second point regards Jesus' admonition to Peter that "all who draw the sword will die by the sword."[18] This isn't just a warning to Peter to stop his attack in order to keep him from being killed. It is also a general statement that those in this world who initiate an armed attack would be dealt with in a like manner. He doesn't go on to bemoan the rightness or wrongness of this; it's simply an acknowledgment of a fact of life.

The sixth commandment, "Thou shalt not kill" must be looked at more closely. The proper translation of the word "kill" is "murder."[19] Some argue that killing in war is indistinguishable from murder, but this is not the case. The premeditated killing of one person by another does not equate with killing in war, where killing is impersonal, commanded by others and necessary to defend a justifiable cause.

The concept of a "just war" defines whether the cause is justifiable. A just war is one in which moral criteria have been used in deciding if, when and how a war is to be waged. It's also a way of determining whether participation in it by Christians is acceptable.

What constitutes a just war? This isn't something that's left to the subjective judgment of whoever is running the government at the time. The concept predates Christianity, going back to the pagan cultures of the Greeks and Romans. It was adopted by St. Augustine, who Christianized the concept. There are no specific guidelines for Christian conduct regarding war in the New Testament, so the idea of a "just war" fills a gap in scripture by detailing Christian responsibilities. It blends Christ's ideals of peace and love with the fact that the world can be a fearsome place where aggressors must sometimes be dealt with militarily.

Very briefly some elements of a just war are that it must:

- *have a just cause (to protect the peace and prevent injury)*
- *have a just intent (restoration of peace; not vengeance)*
- *be a last resort*

- *have a serious prospect of success*
- *be undertaken by legitimate authority*
- *have limited and achievable goals*
- *be proportional (the goal must be worth the cost)*
- *seek to avoid injury to noncombatants and give them immunity*[20]

The New Testament shows Christ to be unwavering in the importance of the core values of love and peace, but it also shows him to be cognizant of worldly forces that threaten those who wish to live in love and peace. Christ wouldn't condemn those who conduct a just war, but would instead see the necessity of defending oneself and one's country in order to preserve or create peace.

People respond to war in different ways. The "fight or flight" instinct causes many to automatically respond to an attack with retribution and little, if any, reflection. Some are pacifists, who disparage any military response and refuse to defend themselves or others. Then there are those who recognize the violent, evil side of humanity and, despite misgivings about war, understand that there are times when an aggressive defense is necessary.

The notion that "peace" is the highest good and that it supersedes all other goals is dangerous. Christians also aspire to promote human dignity and to stand against evil,[21] and these require war when faced by a violent and determined adversary. Inaction due to an idealistic, impractical desire for "peace" in the face of aggression leads only to the ultimate loss of the peace Christians seek to preserve.

Can anyone truly believe that peacefully submitting to Imperial Japan and the Third Reich would have led to a better world? If the Allies had lost the war, freedom would have been eradicated as dictatorships trampled on the concepts of love and peace. This was a time when war was the only path to peace.

History demonstrates that wars sometimes must be fought, and that a pacifist Christian faith that did not allow its adherents to defend themselves would be annihilated. Knowing this, and believing Christians must either be pacifists (and true to their faith) or hypocrites (fighting a war in violation of their faith) led me to believe that Christianity was impractical. This stumbling stone was a factor in my rejecting the faith.

In fact, Christians can—and do—live according to Christ's teachings while keeping a watchful eye on, and a ready defense against, those who would destroy the love and peace they aspire to. And when a war arises they defend their faith, country, and families in good conscience.

14

The Bible

The Bible was written thousands of years ago by people who couldn't have had a clue about what life today would be like. On top of this, it's difficult to read and understand. How could it possibly be relevant to me?

You tip the ladle, pouring molten steel into the mold. Any metal that doesn't hit the inlet solidifies into hot drops that bounce off the mold and cascade back onto you. You're wearing fire-resistant leggings, but sometimes the drops get caught in the clips that hold them onto your legs and you get burned anyway. It's important to get the steel flowing into the mold as quickly as possible because, first, the mold must be filled before the metal freezes and, second, as you choke the metal in faster you can control it better and reduce the spatter.

As the mold is filled, the organic binders that hold it together ignite. This creates smoke that stings your eyes and a pungent odor that bothers your nose. The steel becomes visible in the "risers," holes in the top of the mold that create open pools of metal as the mold fills. Sometimes in mid-pouring, built up gasses detonate with a loud "WHOOMP!!" and a jolt that shakes the floor.

Vents have been cut in the top of the mold to allow gasses to escape. These ignite like torches, shooting flames into the air. With the exposed metal coming up in the risers, the flaming vents, and the fact that you've been hanging onto a 2,500 pound ladle of 3,000 degree molten steel for several minutes, it's getting hot. It's even hotter if you missed badly on your first try and spilled metal that spread out on the floor and radiated heat all the time you've been standing there. Finally, it's done.

You're hot, sweaty, dirty, and enormously satisfied. Most people wouldn't do this job for love or money. A foundryman thinks it's the coolest job in the world.

Johannes Gutenberg, the man who printed the famous Gutenberg Bible, was a foundryman,[1] and his metalcasting know-how led to the development of durable moveable type. Previously, printers used wooden type that wore out after a few copies. Gutenberg's breakthrough was to cast the type in metal so the type lasted much longer, enabling printers to produce large quantities before replacing it.[2] The Bible was the first book printed by this method, and as the new technology spread, so did the Bible. It's the best-selling book of all time and is the best-selling book in the world every year.[3]

The Bible was written by God-inspired writers[4] living in different times and cultures. These authors were from different social and economic positions, including farmer, fisherman, tax collector, carpenter, prophet, soldier, doctor, tentmaker, shepherd, priest and king.[5] Although the dating of the oldest books is debatable, they're estimated by some to have been written circa 1400 BCE. The most recent, "Revelation," was written circa

95 CE, so it took around 1,500 years to compile all 66 books.[6] It was composed by approximately 40 writers and is geographically diverse, with parts written in Africa, Asia and Europe.[7]

The age of the Bible can cause difficulties in understanding it. One problem is that the cultures and customs of ancient times were different from ours, and these are what appear in scripture. The reader's lack of knowledge of these cultural differences can cause misunderstanding. Several examples are:

When Jesus advises you to give a man your cloak,[8] it's important to know that in ancient times cloaks were used for blankets, protection against the weather, carrying sacks, places to sit, and collateral for loans. Clothing was so expensive that most people only owned one cloak.[9]

The term "tearing clothing and wearing sackcloth" refers to a person practicing the customary ritual of mourning.[10] Asherah poles were usually made of wood and erected near altars for the most popular pagan god, Baal. They represented the goddess Asherah, his consort.[11]

Another issue is the misapplication of Biblical verses. A prime example of this is the instruction to exact the punishment of "an eye for an eye and a tooth for a tooth." The common perception is that this promotes revenge, but it actually commands judges to make punishments proportional to the crime. In tempering the barbaric excessive punishments of ancient cultures, it's actually a command of mercy rather than a condoning of vengeance.[12]

Lots of people think the Bible is a collection of stories. To be sure, there are historical narratives and parables that fit this description. But there are a number of issues that can only be understood by looking at passages from various parts of the Bible and putting them together to form the whole picture.

It's like the story of the blind men who each examined a different part of an elephant. One had a leg, one an ear, another the trunk, and the last the tail. Each came up with a wildly different description of what an elephant was. Only by putting together the various descriptions was an accurate portrayal possible. The Bible should be approached the same way, with the understanding that the passages enhance and clarify each other even though they may not appear consecutively. They need to be looked at together to form the complete picture. Heaven, for example, is mentioned in a number of places, and from each of the sources a new aspect is revealed. Following is a partial description composed of elements from several verses:

> It is eternal. —*John 17:2*
> Many who were last will be first. —*Mark 10:31*
> You will be like angels. —*Matthew 22:29*
> You will be with God. —*Matthew 6:9*
> There will be no hunger or thirst. —*Revelation 7:16*
> Every tear will be wiped away. —*Revelation 7:17*
> There will be no death, mourning, crying or pain.
> —*Revelation 21:4*

And there are other passages that touch on the nature of heaven. The point is that there isn't one particular passage that summarizes all of them. The same method must also be used in studying many other issues.

Most of what we know about Jesus is from the New Testament, and it's essential that it be reliable. There are several tests historians use to gauge the credibility of a document. First, they determine the amount of time between the original writing and the earliest existent copies; the shorter the time span the greater the credibility. Second, the number of early copies must be examined; the greater the number of copies the greater the credibility. Examples of ancient writings whose authenticity is accepted are:

Document	Span Between Original Writing and Copies	Number of Copies
History of Thucydides	1,300 years	8
Aristotle's Poetics	1,400 years	5
Caesar's History of the Gallic Wars	1,000 years	10

By comparison, the books of the New Testament were written within 60 years of Christ's crucifixion, and many thousands of remnants exist from the early centuries of the first millennium.[13]

A third test is to determine whether the historical content of the writings are verified by external findings. Archaeological evidence and ancient writings corroborate much of the Bible's text and support its overall trustworthiness. For example, King David was thought by some to have been a fictional character until his existence was confirmed by discoveries in 1993.[14] Similarly, Pilate's position as Roman ruler in Judea at the time of Christ's crucifixion was verified by a finding in 1961.[15] Egyptian records and physical evidence support the existence of Shishak,[16] the first pharaoh mentioned by name in the Bible, and his conquest of Jerusalem. Assyria's King Sargon, whose existence was also questioned, has been "found" by archeology.[17] As more evidence accumulates, the Bible is increasingly validated.

Some skeptics assert that the Old Testament was passed down orally for many centuries before it was written down, and it's nothing more than folk tales that have been embellished over time. This ignores the fact that illiterate ancient cultures routinely transmitted oral accounts accurately over many generations. This is not akin to the party game "telephone," where a message starts at one end of a line and becomes unrecognizably distorted by the time it reaches the last person. Unlike today, when the written word preserves our ideas and we've lost the primacy of oral communication, in ancient times oral transmissions were of necessity memorized and repeated accurately. This process has been found to be working in illiterate communities even today and is known by scholars as "orality" as opposed to "literacy."[18]

The New Testament was written within one generation of the crucifixion, so the idea that the story of Christ was made up or modified like a folk tale isn't credible simply because there wasn't enough time for it to happen. And the existence of thousands of early copies verifying our modern texts confirms the accurate transmission of the original biblical message.

Another issue is the number of Bible translations and the differences between them. The Old Testament was originally recorded in Hebrew and Aramaic; the New Testament was written in Greek. The ancient manuscripts have been used to create a number of different translations in many languages at different times. These updated translations are necessary in order to convey the meanings of the Bible in contemporary terms, because languages are fluid and the meanings of words change over time. For example, in old England when the King James Version was produced, the word "prevent" meant "to come before" but not "to keep something from happening." Because of this, modern translations have changed the word to "precede."[19]

In order to determine the correct meanings of words, it's necessary to go back to the original texts. For example, the New Testament prominently features the word "love," which is its central theme. Our English translations use the word "love" because it's the only one we have. But the New Testament was originally written in Greek, which has numerous words for different types of love: *philia* is affectionate love like that between old friends, *eros* refers to romantic love, and *agape* is unconditional love. Because of this, knowledge of the original Greek word can be essential to the correct understanding of a passage.[20]

In addition to this, various translations are made with different purposes in mind. Some, like the King James Version—which is the most widely circulated translation—is traditional, but more difficult to understand because of the differences in language noted earlier. The New American Standard Bible (NASB) is the most precise English translation, but its tone is academic. The New International Version (NIV) is a contemporary translation that focuses on being true to the original meanings, but it's more easily readable because it doesn't restrict itself to word-for-word translation.[21]

The central question about the Bible is "How can a book written thousands of years ago be relevant to me?" The answer is three-fold. First, it's a study in unchanging human nature that illustrates man's strengths, weaknesses, nobility, dastardliness, selfish desires, selfless sacrifices and every other human trait. Second, it teaches man how to successfully negotiate life and confront problems with practical advice. Third, it informs us about the nature of God.

Sometimes the lessons are direct, as in "Get rid of all bitterness, rage and anger, brawling and slander, along with every form of malice."[22] At other times, the message is delivered in parables that must be interpreted. An example is when Jesus tells a rich young man, "it is easier for a camel to go through the eye of a needle than for a rich man to enter the kingdom of God."[23] The point is that worldly possessions can become idols, superseding faith in God. Since love of possessions is a basic human trait, the disciples were "astonished" and asked, "Who can then be saved?" To which Christ replied, "…with God all things are possible." The lesson is this: even though a man has riches, if his heart is fixed on God and his possessions are secondary in his heart, he can still enter God's kingdom.

God makes himself known through the Bible by his actions and by the teachings of Jesus. God is the creator of the world,[24] can forgive sins,[25] wants to be loved by man,[26] is merciful,[27] doesn't show favoritism,[28] is eternal, immortal and invisible,[29] is the judge of man,[30] avenges evil,[31] knows each individual one of us,[32] and wants man to live by the golden rule.[33] And these are just the tip of the iceberg. Without the

Bible, how could man ever know, in such detail, who God is and what he desires?

It's very difficult to understand many parts of the Bible just by reading the text on your own. There are several ways to overcome this. First, get an edition with explanatory notes. Second, find a church with a pastor who preaches on the Bible rather than on social and political issues. Third, participate in adult Sunday School programs. Fourth, join a small Bible study group that fosters detailed discussion and individual participation.

The Bible is a deep and complex document. It's the ultimate illustration of the expression "the more you know the more you realize you don't know." Despite this—or maybe because of it—its richness and timelessness make it an unsurpassed guide for life.

15

Why Are There So Many Different Christian Churches?

There seems to be a different kind of church on every street corner. They all claim to be Christian, but they often disagree. How can one faith produce such an assortment of views and still be credible?

A Baptist pastor and his wife decided to get a dog and insisted it had to be a Christian dog. They went to a pet store and explained this to the salesperson, who told them this wasn't a problem. He brought out a big, friendly Labrador Retriever and commanded it to "go get the Bible," which the Lab did. He then ordered it to "look up the 23rd Psalm," at which point the dog pawed through the book and stopped at exactly the right page. Duly impressed, the couple bought the dog and brought him home.

Some time later, they were showing off these awesome talents when one of the guests asked if the Lab could follow any regular commands. Not having taught him any new tricks, the pastor decided to take a chance and ordered the dog to "heel!" The Lab promptly stood up on his hind legs, placed a front paw on the pastor's forehead and started crying out.

Taken by surprise, the preacher turned to his wife and exclaimed, "Look at this, Doris—he's a Pentecostal!"

(Pentecostals emphasize faith healing. If you had to read this to get the punchline I apologize for poor joke selection. In a note to my Pentecostal and Baptist friends, please accept that this is just innocent humor and isn't intended to be demeaning or judgmental to either Baptists or Pentecostals).

There are differences in the traditions and beliefs of the various Christian churches. A feature of the Assemblies of God is the practice of healing by the Holy Spirit.[1] Baptists, not surprisingly, emphasize baptism by immersion as a key event that symbolizes the burial of a believer's old life and the beginning of a new one.[2] The Roman Catholic Church traces its beginnings to the disciple Peter, whom they believe Jesus designated as the foundation of the church. Popes, who are said to be successors to Peter, are believed to be infallible in matters of beliefs and morals.[3] Methodists accept the deity of Christ, but believe that the Bible was written by inspired individuals who wrote from their human perspectives. In this view, the Bible is subject to interpretation based on human reason, tradition and experience.[4] Eastern Orthodox Churches regard all of the books of the Bible as the self-revelation of God. Unlike other churches, the Orthodox Churches emphasize the centrality of Christ by enthroning a book containing only the four gospels on its altars.[5] The Eastern Orthodox Church includes the Greek, Russian, Bulgarian, Albanian and other Orthodox Churches, since members take on the names of their nations of origin.[6]

Styles of worship are diverse. Some individual parishes have formal services featuring priests or ministers frocked in resplendent robes with music and pageantry to match. Others are more informal, with pastors dressed in suits accompanied by hymns and spontaneous "amens" from the congregation. Musical expression can include electric guitars, pipe organs, drums, electronic keyboards, tambourines or any other instrument. Traditional hymns, contemporary Christian songs, or gospel music are all used in various churches.

Church buildings can offer hugely different venues for worship. There are spectacular cathedrals throughout the world that leave one with a sense of awe at the dedication and workmanship it took to build them. Many churches in the United States are modest wood frame structures that emphasize the simplicity of both the construction and the message. Others are rented storefronts in tough neighborhoods that don't use architecture as part of the experience, but rely solely on the power of the message itself. There are even tents set up as temporary places of worship by itinerant preachers.

Many individual parishes are not members of larger church organizations. My church, the First Central Baptist Church, has no affiliation with the Southern Baptist Convention, the

American Baptists or any other denomination, and sets its beliefs and mission independently. And even within First Central there are slightly different beliefs among individual members.

The diversity in Christian beliefs and modes of worship has several roots. First, there are cultural differences. Churches that come from the European tradition of large ornate buildings and spectacular pageantry are different from American black churches, which rose from a history of slavery that produced joyful hand-clapping and soulful gospel music. Both of these will be different from churches serving recently arrived Russian immigrants. Many churches are newly formed, small entities that fill niches that weren't being served by existing parishes. The living, changing nature of Christian worship and its constant effort to grow and diversify is nothing short of amazing, especially since it's been happening for two thousand years.

Second, the Bible is a complex book with many teachings and interpretations. Churches latch onto the beliefs that they determine to be the most important and make them their touchstones. Examples of this include the Assemblies of God, for whom spreading the gospel and evangelizing the world are important[7], the Seventh Day Adventists, who believe that prophecy is a gift from God[8], and the United Church of Christ, which strives for unity among the disparate Christian traditions.[9]

Although different churches put more weight on one part of the Bible over another, they all share core beliefs. They all teach that Jesus was the Son of God, he died for our sins, he rose from the dead, our sins are forgiven through his sacrifice and that because of this we can have eternal life in heaven. If they don't believe these things, they are not Christian.

Third, there are genuine differences between the various churches. The Roman Catholic Church believes in the centralized authority of the Pope. The various Orthodox Churches have an Ecumenical Patriarch who is the Archbishop of Constantinople but has no official authority over the autonomous Orthodox Churches.[10] The United Church of Christ gives great independence to individual congregations, each of which decides its actions according to interpretation of the scriptures by its members.[11] The African Methodist Episcopal Church was founded in 1787 by blacks to provide an alternative to segregated churches. It's the first major instance in the Western World of a denomination being formed for sociological reasons rather than theological differences.[12]

There are also fringe groups like snake handlers in pockets of the Appalachians. This sect was started by a bootlegging illiterate preacher named "Little George" Hensley, who taught that you must handle venomous snakes or be condemned to hell.[13] (Hensley ultimately died from a snake bite.) "Little George" misapplied the Bible verse stating that believers shall "take up serpents"[14] and his emphasis on one verse taken out of context demonstrates how dangerously the Bible can be manipulated.[15]

Christian beliefs are sometimes distorted by those of questionable motive, intelligence or mental stability. Perhaps the worst example of this was Jim Jones, a preacher who brought his followers to Guyana, South America. In 1978 he enticed 913 of them to commit suicide by drinking cyanide-laced Kool-Aid.[16] Sects like those at "Jonestown" are run by megalomaniacs who attract the most vulnerable and unquestioning followers who utterly fail to look at their leaders objectively.

A call to Christianity isn't a call to check your brain at the door. It's important for seekers to examine the teachings of leaders critically to determine whether they're in harmony with the basic Christian theme of love, and whether they truly convey the message of the Bible.

The Christian community offers a huge variety of churches to choose from. It's estimated there are 2,500 Protestant denominations,[17] and these don't include the Roman Catholic or Orthodox Churches. It's important to select the right one. In seeking a church, the first step is to evaluate its teachings and then consider secondary issues such as culture and worship style. Participation in the right church is the way a person's faith is developed and reinforced into an ever-growing and lifelong personal support.

Churches have their differences but they're open to everyone regardless of race, sex, social status, wealth, occupation, disability, ethnicity, politics, dress, age, history, success, failure or any of the other things that divide us in the world. They're havens of support, friendship and hope that transcend the hurly-burly of everyday life.

The most important thing—the only important thing—is whether you're able to experience the peace and joy that comes with knowing Christ. If a church doesn't help you do this, then it's not the right place for you.

16

The Crusades, the Inquisition and Other "Christian" Atrocities

Military conquests, pillaging, confiscation of assets, torture, extortion, greed. All have been committed in the name of Jesus Christ. This ugly history exposes the evil nature of Christianity that talk of "peace" and "loving your neighbor" fails to disguise. Remember, actions speak louder than words.

Balboa Park is the jewel of the City of San Diego. Located in the hills overlooking the Pacific Ocean, its lawns, gardens and palm trees are manicured, and the magnificent Spanish style buildings are impeccably maintained. The ambiance is enhanced when the giant outdoor Spreckels Organ is played and the music wafts in the warm sea breezes. A legacy of two international expositions, the park is America's largest urban cultural park and home to 15 museums, the famous San Diego Zoo and several theatres.

I was there on a typical bright, warm, sunny day when I spotted a special exhibit at the Museum of Man. The subject was incongruous with its surroundings. It was entitled "Torture and Intolerance: A History of Torture Throughout the Ages," and it displayed devices of torture and execution used in the Spanish Inquisition. As visitors gawked at the sadistic devices, heavy quasi-religious music played in the background. This was excerpted from the soundtrack of "The Mission," a movie about the Roman Catholic Church's role in the brutal subjugation of South America. The observer got the sense that Christianity was dark, foreboding, treacherous and dangerous.

The roots of the inquisitions extend to Constantine, Emperor of Rome, who converted to Christianity and blended his new beliefs with governmental power.[1] Eventually, heresy (defined as "a deliberate denial of an article of truth of the Catholic faith") became a crime against the state.

In the two centuries prior to the first Inquisition, heresy was regarded as a threat to society, and accused heretics were burned at the stake by mobs. The first Inquisition (there were three) was instituted to address the problem of vigilante justice and create a legal process to control it.[2] The effort became a study in the Law of Unintended Consequences.

In 1231, Pope Gregory IX created the Inquisition, which commissioned tribunals to suppress heresy. The idea was to set up a system that "inquired" about accusations of heresy and deal with them in a legal manner. In practice, inquisitors operated outside of the church hierarchy, were immune from civil authority, and were answerable only to the Pope. They served as prosecutor and judge and, since the last recourse was a virtually impossible appeal to the Pope, they were a law unto themselves. The practices of the Inquisitors included refusing to tell the accused what the charges against him were or who his accusers were, forbidding legal counsel, seizure of the accused's property before conviction, and torture used to extract "confessions." Inquisitors could even charge the dead with heresy, enabling them to posthumously seize their estates from heirs. It was a profitable business since many Inquisitors were allowed to keep the confiscated proceeds for themselves in addition to bribes and fines.[3]

During the 15th century, the government of King Ferdinand V and Queen Isabella focused on creating a united country, and believed this could only be accomplished if the nation was homogeneously Christian. In 1478, the infamous Spanish Inquisition began, when Pope Sixtus IV granted the government of Ferdinand and Isabella authorization for it. This allowed the crown to inquire of alleged heresies and impose punishment on those found guilty. Although Isabella's goal was purification of the population, the practical benefits of seizing private property were clear to others. The Inquisition provided a means of ridding the population of non-Christians, and enabled the government to finance ventures with confiscated wealth instead of raising taxes.[4]

Invoking Christianity in pursuit of these ends, especially by the means used, was an unconscionable perversion of the faith. Secular authorities ignored the teachings of a religion that commanded its followers to love their fellow man, and used the faith as a justification for abusing others.

The crusades were launched for secular reasons while using religion as a pretext. The First Crusade was partially undertaken to stop the Muslims from disrupting Christian pilgrimages to the Holy Land but the crusade had several ulterior motives. Pope Urban II saw the possibilities of (1) Christian control over the Holy Land, (2) reunion of the eastern and western churches, (3) a quelling of disputes between quarrelling European nobles by collectively focusing their aggression on a common enemy and (4) strengthening the papacy.

For almost two hundred years, crusades were mounted to forcibly conquer the Near East. In the end, they failed with a huge cost in human life. Although the crusades sometimes achieved temporary successes, in the end they were beaten back by the relentless Muslims.[5] Pope Urban II's visions remained unfulfilled: the Holy Land stayed under Islamic control, the eastern and western churches remained separate, and the quarrelling nobles turned out to be the vanguard of a European continent bent on periodically immolating itself.

Europe still suffers from cultural hatreds. These are based on secular issues rather than on religion, which covers over the economic and political issues the conflicts are really about. Take Northern Ireland. A seemingly unstoppable terrorist war was waged between the Catholic Irish Republican Army and the Protestants of Northern Ireland into the 1990's. But on May 6, 2000 the IRA put down its weapons and agreed to participate in a negotiated peace.[6] What happened? In the mid-80's Ireland, which had been called "Northern Europe's perennial economic loser," revamped its self-defeating policies and created a dynamic economy with new investment, high productivity, and good jobs. As the country became the "Celtic Tiger" with a bright economic future,[7] the "religious conflict" evaporated. The teachings of Christ had little to do with the conflict, regardless of whether one was on the Catholic or the Protestant side.

The practice of misusing the name of Christ isn't just a European problem. White supremacists in the U.S. belonged to the Ku Klux Klan and terrorized blacks, Jews and other minority groups by threatening, bombing, beating, and lynching their victims. The KKK's symbol? A flaming cross.[8]

Let's pause, take a deep breath, and think about this for a moment.

Critics enjoy citing this history and condemning Christianity. But are we really talking about the teachings of Jesus Christ? Is it possible to believe that Christ's command to love one another resulted in torture, conquest, murder and lynching? Or are these cases of man using his free will to selfishly manipulate institutions and create darkness out of light? The deeds committed by these institutions are stumbling stones to those who think that Christ is somehow responsible for them. In truth, they are irrelevant to a person seeking Christ because we can go back to the source (the Bible) and ignore the false teachings and evil actions that have accumulated since Jesus walked the earth.

The hijacking of Jesus' name to support violent secular agendas is fraudulent, unconscionable and common. The result is that people believe Christianity is the cause of these problems, and they're repulsed by it. This is unfortunate, because Christianity provides a solid framework for a peaceful, loving and workable society. Terror and hate play no part in the Christian message.

If Christianity is seen as morally lacking, we come to the question of where moral standards come from, if not religion. With no biblical guidance, mankind must decide what behavior is acceptable itself. And left on his own, man can be really creative: cannibals eat people, the Aztecs sacrificed humans, and Egyptian pharaohs knocked the noses off the statues of their predecessors to keep them from being able to breathe in the afterlife.[9] Even today, albinos (who suffer from a lack of pigmentation in the skin, hair and eyes) are regarded as bad luck in some primitive cultures, and can be abandoned at birth or killed in ritual sacrifice.[10]

Worse yet is the terror unleashed by political leaders who aren't bound by any moral standards beyond their own megalomania, paranoia and self-interest. You don't have to look far back in recent history to find examples: North Korea, Rwanda, Iraq, Darfur.

By comparison, when Christian nations wage war, the underlying Judeo-Christian moral bedrock helps keep their actions in check. Christian leaders are still human beings, though, and bad things do happen under their rule. The internment of Japanese-Americans in World War II was one of these. But a measure of grace shows through even in this case, since the nation freed them and eventually issued an apology. Can anyone doubt that they would have been unapologetically exterminated in Hitler's Germany, Stalin's Russia, or Mao's China? Contrary to the opinion that Christianity is responsible for heinous behavior, it is a moderating influence.

In the inquisitions and crusades, Christianity was invoked to legitimize agendas that were contrary to Christian ideals. The only way to overcome this is to approach the Bible with an open mind and learn first hand what it teaches. Only then can the sordid history be put in perspective and Christianity correctly understood as a force for tempering man's baser instincts rather than as an agent that inflames the instincts for material and political gain.

Misappropriation of the faith by dishonest aggressors doesn't destroy Christianity's integrity. But it does create a damning impression that can be a serious stumbling stone.

17

Born Agains

Some born again Christians are so giddy with "Jesus" that they seem hopelessly naive. Others insist on telling everybody else how to live. In either case, they put me off.

>Jesus freaks
>Out in the streets
>Handing tickets out for God.
>Turning back
>She just laughs.
>—*"Tiny Dancer," Elton John*[1]

Like Elton John, I saw born again Christians as a sideshow that was amusing unless you were unfortunate enough to have a conversation with one. At that point, their joyful conviction about illogical and impossible beliefs made them more irritating than amusing. Born agains seemed to get along by ignoring life's problems and relying on God to somehow "provide." In their wide-eyed innocence, they exemplified Karl Marx's notion that "religion is the opiate of the masses."[2]

It's important to define what the term means. According to author Wade Clark Roof, many people who call themselves born again do so "because of certain feelings ... and experiences, not because (they) believe any particular set of doctrines."[3] Some believe born agains are out-of-touch fanatics whose principles and beliefs are hopelessly out of step with the modern world. Others see hatred of gays as a defining characteristic, or believe that being born again requires a baptism by immersion. Above all, whatever they believe, born agains are seen to be intolerant, obsessive and pushy.[4]

There are people who fit these descriptions. Their personal views and methods may or may not reflect legitimate Christian points of view but two things are certain. First, they don't reflect the beliefs of all born again Christians because there is no such thing as a politically homogeneous born again movement.[5] Second, when they go on the attack and seek the spotlight they get it. Unfortunately, the attention these people attract from a cynical media distracts attention from what being "born again" really is.

Jesus instructed, "You must be born again."[6] He was speaking of a spiritual rebirth in which a believer commits his life to Christ. Spiritual rebirth is a simple matter, where a person attests to certain beliefs. You must confess that Christ is your savior and Lord and that he rose from the dead.[7] These core beliefs empower the Bible, which, in turn, augments and refines your faith.

Being born again is a spiritual rebirth in which worldly life, with all of its frustration, hurt and ambiguity, is superseded by the certainty of eternal life in the Kingdom of God. Entry into this kingdom is obtainable only if a person believes in Christ and is spiritually reborn. In doing so, the person commits to trying to live his life by the standards of God as exemplified by Jesus. Selflessness is a prominent Christian trait, in contrast to the selfishness that is a fundamental part of human nature. This dichotomy between a believer's aspirations as a Christian and his natural human desires creates a struggle within himself. These flaws will often cause a believer to fail in the struggle to live up to Christ's perfection.

Because of this, Jesus spoke about the hypocrisy of Christians judging others and warned that those who do this would be held to the same standards they applied to others.

He clearly discouraged believers from self-righteous finger pointing.[8] Instead, believers are to refrain from passing judgment and creating impediments to faith.[9]

The fact that Christians are imperfect doesn't disqualify them from trying to persuade others to live by biblical standards. The history of Christianity is replete with believers who were persecuted and killed for spreading the gospel and questioning the conduct of their contemporaries. The key element in acceptable Christian conduct is motive: if a believer's goal is to help a person for the better, then the intercession is justifiable. If the intent is to pass judgment on someone in order to puff oneself up and feed his own ego, then it's wrong.[10]

Christians are in a bind with this issue. Knowing the word of God and the improvement in life it brings compels believers to share their experience with others. Unfortunately, it's easy for unbelievers to see this as a judgmental attempt to foist unwanted beliefs on them. It's a very fine line that, at least as perceived by unbelievers, gets stepped over all the time.

Being born again is about a personal relationship between the believer and God that has nothing to do with politics or society at large. Born agains can have sincere faith and still have differences about worldly matters. That's why Presidents Jimmy Carter and George W. Bush can both be born again but have divergent views on many other issues. The inclusiveness of Christianity is a reason that judgmentalism and condemnation over secular matters is a delicate matter.

Some people think that all born agains must be baptized as adults. While many born again Christians have been through a believer's baptism by immersion, it's not necessary.[11] The key element in spiritual rebirth is the acceptance of Christ in the heart of the believer.[12] This requires nothing more than the believer's sincerity in making a commitment between himself and God. Baptism is a public expression of the believer's commitment, and serves essentially the same purpose as the confirmation ceremonies that are common to many Christian churches. Like confirmation, the ceremony is not necessary to receive salvation, since it's provided by God's grace and individual works—like baptism—aren't requisite.[13]

I was confirmed as a Methodist and later baptized in a Baptist church. I found that there was a huge difference in the personal impact each had. The ritual of baptism, which symbolizes rebirth,[14] was far more meaningful than I ever thought it would be. My wife, Lisa, and I were baptized on Easter Sunday. Along with seven other believers, we were clothed in bathing suits and blue robes that had weights sewn into the hems so they wouldn't float. We were called one by one into the baptismal tank, which was a tub filled with about three feet of warm water. It was located in the front of the church in view of the congregation, with the pastor and assistant pastor already standing in it.

When I was called down the steps into the tank, Pastor Bob Riedy said a few words about me and asked if I would like to say anything about my coming to faith, which I did. After this, the pastor asked if I had "received Christ as Savior and Lord." I answered, "Yes, I have." He then said, "Because of your faith in Christ it is my privilege to baptize you in the name of the Father, Son and Holy Spirit." He held a cloth over my face as I latched my hands onto his forearm and unlocked my knees. He then quickly dipped my head and torso under the water. As he brought me up, the congregation applauded, and the pastor paraphrased a passage from Romans 6:

"We have died with Christ through baptism and, just as Christ was raised from the dead we rise again to live a new life."

In my wet garb I watched my wife and her mother as they were baptized next, then changed into my dry clothes and went to sit in the sanctuary. I spent the rest of the service with my sons, who despite their uncertainty about our newfound faith, had graciously attended.

After the service was over, many of the hundred or so members attending came over to each of the newly baptized Christians and offered handshakes, hugs and congratulations. The spontaneous display of acceptance and joy from the congregation was heartwarming, and emphasized that a bond had been formed between us and other Christians.

Perhaps it was the sincere welcome from the members of the church. Maybe it was relief at having the baptism over with. Possibly it was the aftermath of the slight adrenaline charge that I experienced during the event. Or maybe, just maybe, it was God himself that made this one of the most meaningful and positive experiences of my life. The baptism added gravity to the decision I had made, and emphasized my becoming a believer with an exclamation point.

Like most born again Christians, I don't wear my faith on my sleeve and I try not to impose my beliefs on unreceptive people. On the other hand, if someone shows an interest, I'm delighted to talk about it because the word of God does bring peace, perspective and joy that other things can't.

I finally understand the "Jesus freaks" that Elton John sang about. Although their emotional effervescence will probably never be my style, their motivation and joyful exuberance spring from the same spiritual well as my faith.

18

Christian Charity

Christianity seems to be focused on the individual's relationship with Christ. Is this all about me, or is there more to it?

The tall, slender, elegant spire with its dark gray slate roof sits atop a brick tower. The steeple's height is emphasized by its placement on a hill overlooking the falls on the Chicopee River. The river is spanned by what used to be affectionately known as "the singing bridge" because the deck was originally constructed of steel grating that made an odd whining sound as vehicles passed over it. The bridge couldn't support the weight of modern fire fighting apparatus, so it was rebuilt with concrete. It sings no more.

The church was founded in 1828 by fifteen believers. The congregation met in various facilities, including the Ames Paper Mill, until the current structure was built in 1878. The nearby rivers, the Chicopee and the Connecticut, figured in its history. In the early days some parishioners rowed skiffs across to get to services, baptisms were held in the river, and waterpower ran the mills whose increased employment fueled the church's growth.[1]

It has around 450 members who cross ethnic, racial, social and economic lines. Many active non-members, or "friends" attend church, participate in groups and events, and are welcomed just as if they formally belonged. This is my church, the First Central Baptist Church.

First Central works hard to interact with the community and it hosts a number of programs to do so. The food pantry and clothing closet provide free goods to the needy. The "MOPS" (Mothers of Pre-Schoolers) program offers parenting advice, topical speakers, discussions and a well-deserved break from child rearing to mothers of young children. The quilting group provides instruction and fellowship for women every month.

Celebrate Recovery provides help and support in a group setting for anyone with "hurts, habits and hang-ups" that include addictions, resentment, fear, anger, worry, personal problems and feelings of despair, hopelessness and worthlessness. Additionally, the church offers private individual counseling to members and non-members alike.

Once a month, cash contributions are collected for a discretionary fund used by the pastor to help those who come to the church in need of immediate assistance. When disasters like the tsunami in Asia or Hurricane Katrina happen additional contributions are taken to support the victims. First Central is a mainstay contributor to the Springfield Rescue Mission, which is a local organization that has been helping the hungry, homeless, addicted and poor since 1892.

The church reaches around the world. Missions is the largest appropriation in the church budget, at nearly $150,000.

Funds are disbursed to over forty missions in places like Mexico, Bosnia, Africa, Russia, China, Philippines, and Jamaica as well as Boston, New York City, Chicago and New England.[2]

First Central's activities are impressive but not unique. Americans who worship regularly are 25 percent more likely to make charitable contributions and, when they do, they give almost four times more than secular contributors. They volunteer their time twice as frequently and are twice as likely to donate blood than those who don't attend church.[3]

Christians don't generally contribute their time and money to get a pat on the back or their names in the paper, so it's usually done in a low-key way.[4] They do it because their faith gives them a responsibility to help others,[5] and because it gives them the satisfaction of knowing they're acting in a way that's pleasing to God. As the Bible teaches, we are saved by faith, not works. But "we are God's workmanship, created in Christ Jesus to do good works."[6]

19

The Christian Walk

We all have ideas about what Christian behavior should be, but these are often based on impressions that have little to do with the Bible. How are Christians expected to conduct themselves?

A question was posed in a class I was taking. The question was this: "If Jesus were to take over your body for one day, would anyone notice a difference?" In turn, I asked my son, Drew, if he would notice a difference if Christ took over my body. His immediate response: "Yeah. I'd ask "Who ARE you???.....and what have you done with Dad??"

So it goes in the quest to live like Jesus.

Once a person becomes a Christian he receives eternal life through faith in Christ. Although his salvation is secure regardless of his works, he's obliged to reject sinful behavior and strive to live according to biblical teaching.[1] This may be possible in theory, but in real life it is a real problem. Following is a sampling of some of the things that Christians ideally should do, not do or be:

- *Be merciful.*[2]
- *Give to the one who asks you.*[3]
- *Forgive men who sin against you.*[4]
- *Do not store up treasures on earth.*[5]

- *Do not judge.*[6]
- *Avoid evil thoughts.*[7]
- *Offer "the least of my brothers" food, drink, clothing and shelter.*[8]
- *Avoid arrogance.*[9]
- *Avoid folly.*[10]
- *Do good to those who hate you.*[11]
- *Do everything without complaining or arguing.*[12]
- *Give thanks in all circumstances.*[13]
- *Be kind and compassionate.*[14]
- *Avoid foolish talk.*[15]
- *Do not gossip.*[16]
- *Be patient.*[17]
- *Embrace love, joy and peace.*[18]
- *Do not worry about life or what you will eat or drink.*[19]
- *Avoid envy.*[20]
- *Do not take revenge.*[21]
- *Embrace self-control.*[22]
- *Avoid anger.*[23]
- *Love your neighbor as yourself.*[24]

Prohibitions against murder,[25] stealing,[26] and giving false testimony[27] are also biblical but have been omitted from the list because most of us don't find it difficult to avoid them. The ordinary and commonplace things are what trip us up. In looking at the list two things are evident:

1. We're all human and we all have the tendencies to do wrong things, even though we know what the right things are. If we're honest with ourselves, we'll admit that it sometimes seems like we're programmed to behave in the wrong ways and resisting them takes serious effort.
2. If everyone conducted themselves according to the list, the world would be a better place with patient, kind and merciful people working out their differences in peace and with love.

A third observation is also evident: because the first observation describes our human nature, the second observation will never come to pass. As imperfect people we can't get through a day without falling short in one way or another. This struggle between our sinful natures and the conduct we know is right is what makes the Christian life both impossibly difficult and infinitely rewarding. As an individual embarks on his new life — his "Christian walk"— he progressively modifies his perceptions and behaviors by curtailing the bad and expanding the good. Since this is hard to do in a world that continually beckons to our weak natures, the "walk" is not a leisurely stroll; it's a trek fraught with obstacles. Time after time the temptations will win out but, with effort and God's support, their number and severity will lessen over time.

This process is called "progressive sanctification," and it refers to a Christian gradually modifying his behavior so that his life becomes more like Christ's. Every Christian knows he can never achieve the perfection of Jesus, but the reward is in the effort.

God forgives those who ask for it and repent, even if they have repetitive problems with the same behaviors (which most of us do). Christians wrestle with these issues and become better people because of it. But perfection isn't possible, and life would be awfully frustrating for anyone who believed it was.

Peace, and not exasperation, is the hallmark of a Christian because he knows he's not expected to be perfect, his failings will be forgiven and his eventual place in heaven is secure.

20

The Prism

We hear stories about Christians committing bizarre acts or speaking hatefully in the name of Jesus, and their behavior makes me skeptical. Is there a simple way to know whether they're being true to the teachings of Christ?

To produce stainless steel, raw materials are melted and ten key components are adjusted to make the alloy. Usually the initial "heat" is deficient in one or more elements, but the percentages can be adjusted if the chemistry is determined quickly, while the metal is still molten.

This is done by using a spectrometer. A test sample is poured into a brass mold, and it solidifies quickly. The sample is then zapped by a high voltage charge, releasing a blast of light through a prism that splits the light into its components. Each element emits a slightly different color when burned, and these colors are translated into a readout showing the chemical makeup of the mix. Within minutes, the metal is adjusted in the furnace, and "in spec" metal is poured.

The prism has refined nebulous white light into discrete, meaningful wavelengths. In doing so, it has made it possible for the metal to be "alloyed up" accurately, producing stainless steel that will successfully stand up to corrosive acids.

Correct readings are possible only if the light is diffracted properly, so the prism is the key. If the wrong type is used or the right type is incorrectly oriented, the results will be distorted. The end result will be metal that is defective and possibly dangerous when used.

Christianity is often interpreted through an incorrect prism, or no prism at all. Those who cherry-pick verses from the Bible and use them to justify hate are guilty of this. For example, a group of "Baptists" made news by demonstrating at the funerals of servicemen killed in Iraq, "because their deaths are God's punishment for America's tolerance of homosexuals."[1] They indulged their own hostile predispositions and created a "hateful Christian" sideshow that misrepresented Christianity wherever they went. An Associated Press picture, which was worth at least 1,000 words, was distributed internationally. It showed these "Christians" protesting with signs reading "God Hates You" and "God is Your Enemy." How they could have been thinking about Jesus as they created these signs is beyond comprehension. Unfortunately, wacky episodes like this crop up every so often and they reinforce unbelievers' erroneous views about Christianity.

Christ clearly told us what our prism is. A Jewish religious leader asked him, "Which is the greatest commandment in the Law?" He replied, "Love the Lord your God with all your heart, and with all your soul, and with all your mind.….And the second is like it: Love your neighbor as yourself. All the Law and the Prophets hang on these two commandments." [2]

The Bible is not to be misinterpreted[3] and used as justification for hate with the bogus approval of God. Doing this is like using a spectrometer with a defective prism: the results are wrong, possibly dangerous, and certain to present a distorted view of the faith.

The transcendent Christian value is "loving your neighbor as yourself," and this is the ideal that guides conduct. Filtering thoughts and actions through this prism is the simplest and surest way to know whether behavior is truly Christian.

21

Hypocrisy

I don't know a single Christian who isn't a hypocrite. What does this say about Christians and their faith?

Jimmy Swaggart was raised in the small town of Ferriday, Lousiana with his first cousins, Jerry Lee Lewis and Mickey Gilley. Like them, he was musically talented, but he committed himself to God and took to spreading the Word across the South.[1] For over ten years, he preached in tent revivals while living out of a car with his wife and son.[2] His dynamic, powerful performances led to television. By the 1980's Swaggart was reaching millions of people and bringing in nearly $100 million annually.

In 1987, he denounced televangelists Marvin Gordon and Jim Bakker for their extramarital affairs. In retribution, Gordon hired a private detective to shadow Swaggart and, in the following year, photos were published showing the preacher with a prostitute. In a public confession, Swaggart tearfully admitted his misconduct, asked for forgiveness, and temporarily left the pulpit.[3] His ministry never recovered.

The dictionary defines hypocrisy as "the feigning of beliefs, feelings or virtues that one does not hold or possess."[4] Jimmy

Swaggart certainly fell into this category by criticizing others while engaging in vulgar behavior himself. And he compounded the transgression by taking upon himself God's duty of judgment.[5] He became a laughingstock and a poster child for those who regard Christianity as a religion of hypocrites.

It's easy to find Christians who don't always live up to the ideals that Jesus taught. Only one person was able to achieve a life of perfection, and that was Christ himself. The rest of us are saddled with a self-centered human nature that pushes us to behave in imperfect ways.

Christians are seen as hypocrites because they profess to have high standards but in practice do things that are contrary to those standards. Believers *do* aspire to high standards, but they're in a continual struggle to measure up to them. While particular weaknesses vary from person to person, everyone has some issues they wrestle with.

Those who put down Christians for hypocrisy are able to place themselves on pedestals because they've bought into a morally vague culture. It's easy to casually ignore higher standards when you can invent designer morals to fit individual people and situations. If you're willing to change your standards like you change your socks it's easy to avoid being a hypocrite.

A previous chapter on "The Christian Walk" lists a number of specific behaviors that should be practiced or avoided. Can any of us get through a day and stay in compliance with all of them? I can't, and I don't know anyone who claims they can. But I do know lots of people who recognize their flaws and try to avoid repeating them.

When a Christian falters, he's not necessarily a hypocrite who pretends to hold beliefs he doesn't possess. He's just a believer who's got frailties that prevent him from achieving perfection. And when he falters, he recognizes that what he's done is wrong, he confesses, asks for forgiveness, receives it, gets up, dusts himself off, and moves on.

Bumper sticker wisdom: "Christians aren't perfect—they're just saved." This sounds trite, but it accurately sums up the Christian status. Believers know how hopelessly far from perfection they are, and they readily admit it. But they also know they're assured of eternal life despite their imperfections.

The fact that Christians sin doesn't disqualify them from spreading the Word. Just the opposite is true, since those who know the joy of salvation are its best ambassadors.[6] Most Christians have a sincere desire to share their beliefs with others because of the positive impact their faith has had on them personally.

Exposing others to Jesus doesn't make an imperfect Christian hypocritical. It just makes him a person who cares enough about others to invite them to share in the spiritual rewards he's received.

22

Scientific Perception

Why doesn't science prove there's a God?

✥✥✥✥✥✥✥✥✥✥✥

Per-cep-tion (per-SEP-shuhn) *noun*
1. the act or faculty of apprehending by means of the senses or of the mind; cognition; understanding.[1]

Present an issue and you'll find people who disagree over it. We divide into Democrats and Republicans, conservatives and liberals, adrenaline junkies and couch potatoes, travelers and homebodies, vegetarians and carnivores, just to name a few. These perspectives shade what we see and sometimes predetermine things we're unwilling to see. This affects our perception.

There are open-minded people and closed-minded people. The open-minded are willing to view information and modify their beliefs accordingly, while the closed-minded have set views that they refuse to change, regardless of the evidence.

Albert Einstein was open-minded. As he became convinced of the highly organized nature of the universe, he viewed it as "reason incarnate" and questioned how it came to be. His answer, like the answer of many other scientists, was the Mind of God. He famously stated, "I want to know how God created the world…I want to know His thoughts. The rest are details." Despite his belief in God, he has repeatedly been cast as an atheist, a charge he denied by stating "I'm not an atheist" and "What really makes me angry is that they [people who say there is no God] quote me for support of their views."[2]

Einstein's reliance on mathematical perfection and scientific observation led him to accept God as the creator and organizer of the universe. Unfortunately, his dogged dependence on empirical evidence evidently prevented him from taking the step into faith in a God who could answer prayers and offer an afterlife.[3] Since God's presence is most dramatically seen by those who've gone beyond hard science and added a spiritual dimension to the things they perceive, it's not surprising that the personal God would be unseen by Professor Einstein.

There are a number of scientific arguments regarding God's existence that illustrate the unwillingness to break with atheistic paradigms. Consider the creation of life according to evolutionary theory. Before life existed, the earth consisted of inanimate materials like rock, hydrogen, metal ores and water. Life was somehow born out of this lifelessness. Scientists are pretty sure Dr. Frankenstein wasn't present and that he didn't pull a switch to animate the first life-form, so it's accepted that some unknown event is responsible. Although science is at a loss to explain how this happened, God isn't even regarded as an option.

DNA is present in all of life. It provides the mechanism for transmitting characteristics of species between generations and the operating instructions that enable each individual to function.[4] Without its activity in replicating cells and passing on genetic information, life wouldn't exist.

Its complexity, even in simple cells, is enormous. Blue-green algae is the earliest form of life found in fossils, it's common on Earth today[5] and it's been studied exhaustively. Researchers have found that its DNA possesses 6.4 million base pairs (these are the rungs on the double helix ladder)[6] and 5,368 genes.[7]

The algae is relatively complicated compared to its simpler predecessors, but even these first cells would have required a "long and complex molecule." And it would have had to overcome the fact that DNA can't be synthesized without complex proteins that, in turn, can't be formed without the DNA. It's a "Which came first, the chicken or the egg?" problem.[8]

A team from the University of Colorado and the University of Milan was able to coax tiny fragments of DNA to combine with each other in an effort to find a way "for simple molecules to spontaneously self-select, chain-up and self-replicate." But they needed to start with existing DNA and stated that "the formation of molecular chains as uniform as DNA by random chemistry is essentially impossible."[9]

Science doesn't have an explanation for the leap from inanimate material to live organisms,[10] so disbelievers in God "invoke the magic of large numbers" and claim that life only needs to arise on one of billions of planets and so, given the odds, it must have happened randomly and Earth was the lucky winner.[11] Nobel Laureate physiologist George Wald once confessed that "we choose to believe the impossible: that life arose spontaneously, by chance."[12] He later agreed with philosopher Antony Flew that "The only satisfactory explanation for the origin of such end directed, self-replicating life as we see on earth is an infinitely intelligent mind."[13] Incidentally, Flew was a renowned atheist until the weight of the scientific evidence eventually brought him to belief in God.[14]

The "magic of large numbers" has been illustrated by the "monkey theorem" which postulates that if monkeys were placed in a cage with typewriters for a long enough time, they would eventually turn out a Shakespearean sonnet. The British National Council for the Arts took the theorem to task and put six monkeys together with a computer. After a month of abusing the keyboard, they produced 50 pages, but no words (including the word "a," which just needed spaces on each side to qualify).

The mathematical probability of this working out randomly is staggering. Let's say there are 30 keys on a keyboard. In order to form the word "a," three spaces (2 blank spaces plus the letter "a") must be used. This means the probability is 30 x 30 x 30, or one in 27,000, to type it. To produce a 488 word sonnet, the probability is ten to the 690th power, or 10 followed by 690 zeroes, which is more than eight times the estimated total number of protons, neutrons and electrons in the universe. The notion that this is possible is "absurd."[15]

Producing a sonnet is child's play compared to assembling DNA. Even if the raw materials were present, the "chicken and the egg" conundrum solved, and the double helix created, the problem of investing it with life would still be unanswered.

Other topics include the sources of consciousness and thought. The brain is essentially a system of neurons that perform functions according to directions, much like a computer. The question is where the instructions come from. The neurons in your brain don't decide it's time to balance your checkbook. You (your conscious self) decide and put your brain to work figuring it out.[16]

Functionalists (who theorize "that mental states or processes are just identical to some particular brain states or processes")[17] try to explain that machines, such as our brain, "can be conscious because we are machines that are conscious."[18] In other words, "I believe I am a machine. I am conscious, therefore machines can be conscious." This line of thinking has critics even among academics like Stephen Pinker, an experimental psychologist at Harvard. When asked where consciousness comes from and what the explanation for it is, his response is "Beats the heck out of me."[19] Philosopher John Searle of the University of California at Berkeley is even more to the point, noting "If you are tempted to functionalism, I believe you do not need refutation, you need help."[20]

On the other hand, a believer has the option of simply understanding that he has a soul that was given to him by God, and this is his consciousness.

The "Brights" is a term used by persons who subscribe to "a naturalistic worldview" "free of supernatural and mystical elements."[21] In other words, they're atheists. People like this see science as the source of truth. Let's turn the tables and look at their "truth" as skeptically as they do our faith.

Dedicated scientists have increased knowledge and improved life in countless ways. They're rightly honored and appreciated. But science also has a hidden underbelly that can work against truth.

Private foundations, university endowment funds, industries, governments and others all fund research, and their biases are reflected in the projects they choose to support. Researchers need to submit studies that will attract the money[22] and pro-faith projects are seldom approved by overwhelmingly secular funding sources. This reality subtly restricts the scope of inquiry even before studies are proposed.

Dishonesty is a problem. Dr. Marc Hauser, Ph.D. of Harvard University was a star in the field of evolutionary psychology who tried to show that morality is the result of evolutionary processes. He cooked the data, was exposed by his assistants and the fraud was publicized.[23] Here's the amazing thing: the government – not Harvard – made it public because Hauser used federal money.[24] If he hadn't, the misconduct would probably still be unknown outside of academic circles because universities handle these cases internally and try to avoid airing their dirty laundry in public.[25] Openness doesn't suit anybody's purpose, so problems are handled quietly. "Breakthroughs" are trumpeted, retractions aren't (if they're issued at all) and the public is clueless.

Sometimes "science" is conjectural. Evolutionary researchers Randy Thornhill and Craig Palmer wrote *A Natural History of Rape* which was published by The MIT Press. As is typical in their field they based their research largely on animal and insect behavior and claimed rape is simply a natural product of evolution.[26] After receiving national news attention, they were vehemently denounced by anti-rape activists[27] and other scientists who supported the critics.[28]

Nobody noted that (1) this sort of study is fraught with speculation, intuition and guesswork, and (2) neither side is either testable or even knowable. In the end, the "scientific" controversy was settled in the court of public opinion.

And then there's the manipulation of statistics…we could go on…

Here's an astonishing fact: even in a hard science like biology over 64% of published results can't be replicated.[29] You have to wonder how much egotism, bias, incompetence, carelessness and dishonesty there is in the scientific community for this to be true. You also have to wonder how much truth the soft sciences produce, where evidence is mushier than in biology.

When studies from soft sciences like sociology, psychology, evolutionary psychology and others dispute time-tested biblical teaching we should ask some questions: "Who paid for it?" "Who designed and interpreted it?" "What are their biases?" and especially "Does the conclusion make sense?" It's amazing how often it doesn't.

We shouldn't be intimidated by fancy credentials. People with doctorates often inhabit academic echo chambers that perpetuate anti-faith prejudices, and advanced degrees don't certify a grasp of common sense. They can be wrong and we shouldn't unquestioningly accept them at face value.

By its nature scientific knowledge changes, it can be subjective and it's vulnerable to human weaknesses. This gives the "naturalistic worldview" a flawed foundation.

At any rate, the purview of science is to examine the universe and learn how it works. Nuclear physics, quantum mechanics, molecular biology, computer electronics, oceanography and thousands of other fields are constantly studied to expand our understanding and increase our ability to use natural processes for our own ends. But science is limited in its ability to explain where this order came from.

Science is able to function because the universe is meticulously organized, from the way atoms are assembled to the forces that keep the solar system synchronized. These detailed, complex systems can be theorized to have come about by chance or they can be seen to be the handiwork of a maker. Here's a simple question: did the watch on your wrist—which is relatively simple object—just randomly appear, or was it made by an intelligent being with an organized plan? The answer is obvious. Isn't it fair to ask the same question about a universe that is infinitely more complicated than your wristwatch? Isn't the answer equally obvious?

Spirituality—especially Christian spirituality—is disdained by those who don't understand it and refuse to even try. This bias can cause skeptics to dismiss the idea that God is the creator out of hand. But there are many scientists with open minds who see the Mind of God in the workings of creation and who have come to faith because of it. In fact, a survey of biologists, physicists and mathematicians found that about 40% "believed in a God who actively communicates with humankind and to whom one may pray."[22] Unfortunately, they don't get attention like the cynics and we're given the false perception that the scientific community is universally skeptical about the existence of God.

In the end, whether science proves God's existence depends on who is viewing the evidence. Even those who rely solely on empirical evidence but who have open minds, like Albert Einstein, see God. Those who close off God up front don't see him because they refuse to. In TV programs, textbooks, museums, the media in general, and other politically correct venues,[23] the central player in all of existence is missing. And by this absence we're given the subtle, false message that science has determined God isn't necessary and doesn't exist.

23

Creation

Science has shown that the universe was formed over billions of years, but the Bible claims it was done in less than a week. How is it possible to accept the Bible's version?

The Lord of the Rings trilogy by J.R.R. Tolkien is set in an imaginary place called Middle-earth. Frodo Baggins has been given the Ruling Ring. The ring is hotly pursued by Sauron, the Dark Lord, because it would enable him to rule all. Baggins must undertake a dangerous mission to destroy the evil ring by casting it into the fires of Mount Doom before it's captured by its pursuers.[1]

Middle-earth is a mythical place with extreme features. After an extensive search for a location, the movie's producers chose a spectacular venue with pristine lakes, unspoiled plains and snow-capped mountains. They selected Tongariro National Park in New Zealand, with volcanic Mount Nguaruhoe visible in the distance.[2]

Mount Nguaruhoe hadn't erupted in some time. Geologists found that lava flows had occurred between 270,000 and 3.5 million years ago, so it appeared to be a safe time to film here. Or was it? Unlike most long-age datings, the scientifically determined timing of these eruptions was disputed by current residents who watched them happen. In fact, one flow had occurred in 1949, three in 1954 and one in 1975.[3]

Dating discrepancies like this cause heated debates between geologists, who believe the Earth is the result of natural processes that occurred over millions of years, and biblical creationists, who are convinced it was created by God only a few thousand years ago. The creationist and the geologic dating communities disdain each other, producing a debate that's somehow dry and inflammatory at the same time. Rather than get bogged down in their arguments, let's find out if there's any agreement between science and the Bible regarding creation.

Following is a comparison of the biblical creation story and scientific thought, with each step in the creation process listed in sequence. The Bible verses have been paraphrased, and complex scientific concepts have been summarized, but the substance of each is accurate.

Day 1: The heavens, earth, light, "day" and "night" are created.[4]

Beginning with Aristotle, thinkers believed matter was eternal, and that no creation event ever occurred.[5] This thinking held sway until the 20th Century, when astronomer Edwin Hubble observed that the universe is continually expanding.[6] The corollary to this is that the galaxies started in one place, where all matter was compressed into such an infinitely small point that it ceased to exist. This condition of nothingness is where the universe theoretically began.

Earlier, Albert Einstein had developed equations that came close to mathematically proving the expanding nature of the universe, but they fell short. In reviewing Einstein's work, mathematician Alexander Friedmann discovered a simple error in the original calculations. When the correction was made, the equations confirmed the theory. At first, Einstein was reluctant to believe his calculations because of their huge implications. But in the end, faced with the strength of his own work and Hubble's findings, he relinquished his long-held beliefs and conceded that the universe did have a beginning.[7]

The dispelling of belief in a "no creation" universe prompted the development of the Big Bang Theory. The Big Bang Theory hypothesizes that the universe initially existed in a single point of such incredible density that neither energy nor matter existed. In an inconceivably powerful explosion, radiation emerged that was so intense matter could not form. As the energy cooled, electrons matched up with other elements of atoms, and eventually created stars, galaxies and the solar system that includes Earth. There are many differences between Earth and its fellow planets, but two are particularly relevant to the creation story. Earth's unique attributes were (1) a higher allotment of water-forming compounds which enabled it to generate massive amounts of water and (2) a distance from the Sun which made it possible for the water to exist as a stable liquid rather than ice or steam.[8] In a process called outgassing, the water trapped in the Earth's rocks was vaporized into the atmosphere, where it cooled and condensed into water. The water formed a sea that covered the entire planet.[9]

Scientists theorize that the first emanations from the explosion were photons, also known as radiant energy, also known as light. Light was a dominant feature of the Big Bang, just as it's a dominant feature of the Genesis account.[10]

Another feature of Earth that makes the existence of water possible is the twenty-four hour rotation on its axis. If Earth rotated more slowly, water would either vaporize or freeze, depending upon whether it was exposed to the Sun or located on the dark side. This timing is not typical: Venus, a planet roughly the size of Earth, rotates only once every eight months. The timing of the rotation creating night and day is critical to Earth's ability to support life.[11]

Summary of scientific theory:

The universe is created in a blinding blast of light. Earth, covered in water, is created. Day and night are created as a result of the Earth's rotation.

Day 2: An expanse, called "sky" is created to separate water under the expanse from water above it.[12]

As a result of outgassing, the earth was enveloped in a massive, dense black cloud consisting of water vapor and smog-like gasses. Outgassing was caused by volcanic eruptions that spewed water vapor and gases that helped maintain a hot temperature on the surface of the planet.[13] At first, this heat quickly vaporized any rain that fell, but eventually the Earth's crust cooled enough for water to accumulate on the surface. As this cooling progressed and volcanic activity subsided, water formation was stabilized. This resulted in the recycling of water through the atmosphere. In other words, the "sky" was created as a separation occurred between liquid water on the surface and water vapor contained in high altitude clouds.[14]

Summary of scientific theory:

An atmosphere is created that separates the water (vapor) in the heavens from the (liquid) water on the surface.

Day 3: The land and the seas are created; the land is vegetated.[15]

According to geologists, the interior of our planet is in a hot, semi-molten state which was initially homogeneous. Over time, lighter granitic rock rose to the surface while heavier basaltic rock remained lower. The lighter rock broke through the surface of the water that cloaked the Earth and formed the continents, while the heavier rock became the ocean floors.[16]

Science postulates that around the same time the land and seas were being created, life in the form of blue-green algae appeared. The algae eventually developed into more complicated plants in the wetlands and then into seed-bearing plants and trees. Through photosynthesis, the vegetative life transformed the atmosphere from a makeup of dense carbon dioxide and noxious gases into an oxygen-rich mixture conducive to animal life.[17]

Summary of scientific theory:

Lighter rock pokes through the water, creating land and seas. The land is vegetated.

Day 4: Lights in the sky are created which separate day from night, mark time and provide light on the Earth.[18]

The sun, moon and stars that had not been visible from Earth were exposed as the thick fog dissipated. The sun became the "greater light to govern the day" while the moon was the "lesser light to govern the night." The movements of the Earth and moon created a way to "mark seasons and days and years."[19]

As a result of photosynthesis, lethal ultraviolet rays were screened out by the creation of an ozone layer. The light provided by the sun was transformed from being a killer to becoming a source of energy usable by advanced life on Earth.[20]

Summary of scientific theory:

As the thick atmosphere thinned, the sun, moon and stars appear. Beneficial light is allowed through the new atmosphere.

Day 5: The "creatures of the sea" and birds are created.[21]

The term "Cambrian explosion" refers to the sudden appearance of complex, multi-cellular and fully formed creatures in the waters of Earth. In short order, invertebrate animals such as sponges, jellyfish, and mollusks appear. They're followed by vertebrate fishes, which enter the record during the Age of Fishes, and cause the seas to abruptly teem with new organisms. Later, birds enter the scene.[22]

Summary of scientific theory:

Creatures of the sea appear and, later, birds appear.

Day 6: All the creatures that move along the ground, livestock and wild animals appear; man is created.[23]

Mammals inhabited the Earth after the creatures of the sea and the birds. In a fashion similar to the Cambrian explosion, a burst of new life forms involving all of the basic forms of mammals occurred. Scientists call this the explosive adaptive radiation of the mammals. Man appears after this.[24]

Summary of scientific theory:

Land animals enter the scene and man appears afterward.

Day 7: Creation has been completed.

Science and the Bible agree on the steps of creation and their order.

There are other points to consider. Perhaps the most important is that there are two ways of looking at creation. The first is the closed system view, which postulates that everything must be explained within a box containing only that which is observable by man. Everything in the cosmos is included, and anything that happens within it must be explained by elements within it.[25]

The other paradigm is the open system view. Like previous scientists, including Copernicus, Galileo, Francis Bacon and Isaac Newton,[26] adherents to this view see the same elements in the box, but believe there is an entity outside the box that can, and does, affect things in it.[27] This entity is God.

The Big Bang Theory's weakness is its difficulty in explaining how or why the explosion started. Closed system theorists, who by definition must exclude God from their thinking, have conceived the "ekpyrotic model." The idea is that the universe forever alternates between expansion resulting from a "big bang," and a contraction ending in a "big crunch," in which all matter is once again crushed into its pre-big bang state. Once it's crunched, the "big bang" happens all over again. This sounds suspiciously like Aristotelean notion of "no creation" that was in vogue until Einstein and Hubble disproved it. The scientific community disputes the "big crunch" theory by calling its mathematics "half-baked," referring to it as a "step backwards," and questioning "why physicists needed to develop such a bizarre alternative."[28] It seems to be a case of some scientists tying theories into knots in order to stay within their closed system.

If we view our existence as an open system, the problem disappears. We accept that the universe was created out of nothingness and God made it happen.

And then there's Moses, the writer of Genesis. Is the accuracy of his account just the result of lucky guesses by a nomad wandering in the Sinai Desert, or is it due to the direction and guidance of God? If the former is the case, why would he think that the universe began with light, that Earth was completely covered by water and land rose out of it later, or that sea creatures predated land creatures? It took 3,500 years for science to reach these conclusions, and yet Moses got it right without telescopes, advanced mathematics, or any other scientific input.

Arno Penzias is a Nobel Prize-winner who co-discovered background radiation that helped confirm the Big Bang. He states, "The best data we have are exactly what I would have predicted, had I nothing to go on but the five Books of Moses, the Psalms, (and) the Bible as a whole."[29]

Open system adherents explain simply that Moses got the information from God, while the closed system view must chalk up his accuracy to chance. Which scenario makes sense?

A point of contention among Christians is whether the term "days" is used in a literal sense or not. If it denotes ages, the Genesis creation story dovetails with established scientific theory. If it means twenty-four hour days, the sequence still agrees but the time element doesn't. People with faith in the shorter period believe their view will eventually be vindicated as science progresses. After all, it took science many centuries to figure out the universe even *had* a creation!

The lessons to be drawn from all of this are as follows: First, the Bible is unchanging and steadfast in its account of creation. Second, scientific knowledge continually changes. Third, science took a huge leap toward agreement with the Bible when it finally agreed there actually was a creation, and then went on to develop theories about the nature of the process that supported the biblical account. Looked at objectively, without an anti-religion closed-system bias, the evidence points to God the Creator.

24

Evolution

The teaching of evolution in schools is an issue that never goes away. We see news articles about discoveries that support the Theory of Evolution and television shows that explain how man developed. Christians look ignorant when they fight this battle. Why don't they give it up?

In the early 19th century, a Frenchman named Jean Baptiste de Lamarck proposed a concept he called "transformism,"[1] which theorized that complex organisms develop incrementally from simpler organisms over long periods of time. Although de Lamarck died in obscure poverty without his work being taken seriously,[2] his ideas enthused Charles Darwin, the son of an English physician and naturalist. Darwin initially studied medicine, but quit because the practice of surgery without anesthesia repelled him. Instead, he attended Cambridge University where he became a divinity student.[3] He also informally studied with Charles Lyell, the great geologist.

At 22 years old, he was chosen to be the unpaid naturalist on the voyage of the HMS Beagle in 1831.[4] One of the Beagle's missions was to survey the coasts of South America from Brazil, around the cape, into Chile. While rounding Cape Horn, the crew survived storms in the treacherous Straits of Magellan, encountered cannibals,[5] and engaged in a skirmish with natives.[6] The ship also stopped at Cape Gregory, where Darwin interviewed "gigantic Patagonians," who were six feet tall and sported red and black painted faces.[7]

On a voyage that circumnavigated the globe, the most significant observations were made in the South Pacific, on a bizarre volcanic archipelago called the Galapagos Islands. According to Darwin, the craters on the larger islands rose three to four thousand feet and there were at least two thousand craters in all.[8] The islands were inhabited by "aboriginal creations" found nowhere else. As Darwin wrote, it is "a little world unto itself."[9]

The islands were located within 60 miles of each other but were separated by strong currents that prevented species from mingling from island to island. Its climate was remarkably free of gales which reduced the opportunity for insects, birds and seeds to be blown to different islands. This unusual environment enabled organisms to develop independently of each other.[10]

He observed, noted and collected various species of flora and fauna, but the most noteworthy creatures were at least six varieties of finches which were differentiated by the sizes of their beaks. Darwin speculated that these variations had arisen from one original species, whose traits had been modified for different purposes[11] over time. Some twenty years later, he published *On the Origin of Species by Natural Selection*, which explained the process that enabled differences like those between the finches to occur, and seemed to provide the answers to "how" and "why" de Lamarck's "transformism" worked. Species were modified through "natural selection," which enabled those with traits that worked best in their particular environment to succeed and reproduce more effectively. Stronger, better adapted individuals survived and passed their traits on to the next generation, creating progressive adaptations that enhanced the prospects for the long term survival of the species.[12] Given very long periods of time, the process could result in organisms that varied tremendously from their progenitors.[13]

Evolutionists like Richard Dawkins postulate that life began in a "chemical event or series of events" and that "once the vital ingredient—some kind of genetic molecule—is in place, true Darwinian natural selection can follow, and complex life emerges."[14] Many Christians take issue with this. As noted by researcher Francis Collins, they "believe that all species were created by individual acts of divine creation…and not descended from other creatures."[15]

The creationists have arguments to support their views. They point to Darwin's book, in which he devoted four chapters to what he called "the most apparent and gravest difficulties on the theory."[16] One of these difficulties lies in his statement that "if my theory be true, numberless intermediate varieties, linking closely together all the species of the same group, must assuredly have existed."[17] This means that unlike the drawings that depict modern man emerging at the end of a chain of six or seven progressively more human creatures, there would be huge numbers of intermediary creatures reflecting many thousands of tiny changes. Darwin knew there were huge intervals in the fossil record and that the existing evidence didn't support his theory.[18] Despite the research that has been done since the book was published in 1859, large gaps (periods where there are no transitional forms between different varieties) still exist. As renowned Harvard paleontologist and evolutionist Stephen Jay Gould remarked, "The extreme rarity of transitional forms in the fossil record persists as the trade secret of paleontology."[19]

Darwin also noted that the development of "Organs of extreme perfection and complication" cause difficulty with the theory. An organ discussed by Darwin was the eye. It was hard to envision that countless unrelated changes could be made over millions of years and finally come together to produce a fully functioning eye. The improbability of this happening was expressed by Darwin when he wrote "To suppose that the eye could have been formed by natural selection, seems, I freely confess, absurd in the highest degree."[20]

Creationists argue that what Darwin's observations show is not necessarily evolution, but adaptation. Adaptation refers to changes that happen within a species to make a particular branch of that species different and better able to survive.[21] We see these types of modifications even on a short term basis. For example, in the 1930's and 1940's, a lake in Washington State was stocked with sockeye salmon. After 60 years researchers discovered that some of the fish had migrated to a river that fed the lake and adapted to it by developing slimmer, more streamlined bodies that made them more hydrodynamic in the fast water.[22] No one disputes that species undergo modifications like this, and man has used the process himself for thousands of years by breeding animals and cultivating plants to achieve desired traits.

The difference between adaptive changes, such as the differences in the sockeye salmon or the beaks of Darwin's finches and evolution is that evolution would have one believe that these traits signify a movement toward creating a new species fundamentally different from its predecessors.[23] Differentiations happen within the same species all the time. For example, there are hundreds of breeds of dogs, not counting the mutts, and they have significant differences between them, but no one would dispute that they're all still dogs. We don't see dogs gradually turning into goats or any other non-dog species.

This type of transformation would have to be routine in order to achieve the incredible varieties of separate species that theoretically developed from simple origins millions of years ago. To skeptics of evolution, the notion that "evolution means that we're all distant cousins: humans and oak trees, hummingbirds and whales"[24] is nonsensical.

The public perception that evolution is beyond question is partly due to the routine portrayal of adaptation as proof of evolution. The story about the fish in the river was presented in exactly that fashion. Since people can see that adaptation happens, equating it with evolution leads to an almost automatic acceptance of the theory.

But some species defy easy answers, like the tiny Hawaiian goby. Offspring hatch in pools at the top of the highest waterfall on the Big Island but are soon swept down to the sea. The survivors make their way back up using suckers to attach themselves to a wet waterfall cliff hundreds of feet high. Then they flap their little tails in bursts to push themselves to the top where the process begins again.[25] It's hard to see how this amazing exercise could have developed in minute steps over eons. God's probably wryly smiling and thinking, "It's my work. Open your eyes!"

Evolution theoretically begins in what's called a "primordial soup." It's said that billions of years ago, a watery mixture contained chemicals that randomly arranged themselves into a molecule that was able to reproduce itself, thus starting the evolutionary chain. In a famous experiment in 1953, Stanley Miller of the University of Chicago sent an electric current through an artificially created atmosphere of the prebiotic (existing before the origin of life)[26] earth and found it produced most of the amino acids and other components required for life, although some were unstable.[27] This result has been used to support the idea of the spontaneous creation of life, even though no one has been able to actually generate all of the needed elements and then instill life into the mix. Granted, the amount of time since the experiments were first done is insignificant compared to the billions of years that evolutionary theory presumes. But no matter what length of time is available, creationists think it's a pipe dream to believe that all of the necessary elements of life could randomly assemble in the same place, at the same time and that a mysterious life force could then simultaneously animate them. (Sidebar: Why do evolutionists freely put their faith into a life-giving force as long as it's not called God?).

Heroism is another problem raised by Darwin. The ultimate heroism is sacrificing one's life to save the lives of others and it's one of mankind's noble traits. When we see it, we exalt it. It's the reason the FDNY rescuers on 9/11 will be proud fixtures in the American psyche forever. And it's common to humanity. Although most of us deny we could be heroes, the most unlikely and ordinary people exhibit heroism when the circumstances present themselves. But self-sacrifice doesn't fit with evolution, which insists that survival of the self and the passing along of an organism's personal genes is the ultimate purpose of life. In the evolutionary scheme of things, what could prompt a species to develop and pass on a trait that was likely to kill off the individual and reduce the chances that his genes could be passed on?[28]

The development of brain imaging techniques has brought with it the field of "neurotheology," which studies the activity of the brain during spiritual experiences and tries to attribute religious experiences to the wiring of the brain rather than to God.[29, 30] You'd think evolutionists would expect that this particular trait appeared in man for good reason, just as all the other modifications developed for a purpose. But it's hard to envision a rationale for man evolving a mechanism for religious experiences when God doesn't even exist in the evolutionary scheme of things. To skeptics of evolution it's apparent that man was created this way in order to enable him to experience a relationship with a real and existing God. What else could its purpose be?

The Moral Law is a term for the innate sense of right and wrong that exists in man, regardless of the time or culture into which he's born. This universal sense includes "denunciations of oppression, murder, treachery, falsehood (and) injunctions of kindness to the aged, the young and the weak, of almsgiving and impartiality and honesty."[31] It's the characteristic that compels us to perform a selfless act with nothing more to gain than the satisfaction of doing the right thing.[32] The behaviors encouraged by the Moral Law are altruistic and good: just the sort of thing God would instill. Bare-knuckled evolution has a problem in explaining this, too, since altruism is the opposite of survivalism.

Creationists assert that their beliefs aren't challenged by scientific facts, since the evidence demonstrates there are gaps between episodes of creation that coincide with the biblical account of creation. To try to reconcile the evolutionary theory with the evidence, agnostic Stephen Jay Gould[33] and Niles Eldridge postulated the "Theory of Punctuated Equilibrium." This proposed that long periods of evolutionary stability were periodically interrupted by spurts of radical change.[34] On the one hand, it eliminates the necessity of finding transitional forms. On the other hand, the idea that one species could remain unchanged for long periods and then suddenly morph into another seems preposterous. Creationists contend that the evidence requires mental gymnastics like this in order to reconcile the theory with the facts.

Underlying the battle over creation is the notion that the Theory of Evolution is hopelessly related to religion or, more to the point, to anti-religion. As evolution is increasingly accepted creationists see it as an effort to threaten and contradict their faith, and with good reason. Strident atheistic evolutionists like Richard Dawkins and Daniel Dennett go out of their way to try to tear down religion.[35] Each side has its arguments, neither sees any grounds for compromise, and the quarrel goes on.

There are Christians who believe in both evolution and God. Dr. Francis S. Collins is a Christian and former atheist who became head of the Human Genome Project, a ten year effort that mapped the total DNA sequence for humans. This provided "a vast instruction book" that includes "the parts list for human biology" and "clues to a long list of diseases."[36]

Dr. Collins came to the conclusion that science and faith are harmonious, with science explaining the natural world, and faith explaining a spiritual world that's beyond the scope of scientific inquiry. Evolution is seen as initiated by God as part of the creation process. God participates in the process by, for example, imparting spiritual traits into mankind[37] that cannot otherwise be the result of pure, survivalist evolution. These traits include altruism, heroism, and the ability to experience a relationship with God. In accepting the presence of God in the process, we open ourselves to comprehending "the meaning of life, the reality of God, the possibility of an afterlife, and many other spiritual questions"[38] that are beyond the scope of mechanistic evolution.

Biblical texts "carry the clear marks of eyewitness history, and as believers we must hold fast to those truths."[39] But passages regarding the natural universe are regarded as "intended to instruct readers of Moses' time about God's character, and not to attempt to teach scientific facts."[40] After all, the Bible is a spiritual guide, not a natural history primer.

Scientific discovery neither negates the Bible nor threatens faith. A similar situation existed in the 1600's, when Galileo concluded that the earth circled the sun. This conflicted with the Catholic Church's interpretation of the Bible and landed the astronomer under house arrest for the last nine years of his life. Today a heliocentric solar system is common knowledge, and faith remains unharmed.[41]

The complementary melding of science and faith is called theistic evolution, and it "is the dominant position of serious biologists who are also serious believers."[42] For adherents, it provides a framework that blends evolution with faith and removes the venom from the discussion.

The origin of life can't be explained by evolution unless we're willing to accept Richard Dawkins' assessment that life just happened to appear on one of a "billion billion" planets. Remember the monkeys typing Shakespeare in Chapter 22? There are over 38 times the number of zeroes in that probability than there are in a billion billion. It is sophistry to pretend that in practical terms the chances of the random, undirected generation of life is anything over zero.

The controversy won't go away, but one point is clear. The creation of life is in the realm of faith. Whether one believes God created all creatures in separate episodes of creation, or sees his hand in the complex workings of DNA and the spirituality of man, God is indispensable in understanding our presence on Earth.

25

A False Choice

Science disputes faith.
Why would anyone believe faith over fact?

    A false choice presents two solutions to a problem, neither of which is correct. For example, we may think science and faith are opposite, adversarial versions of the world and we've got to choose one over the other. It's a false choice that clouds the real answer.

    It wasn't always this way. Up until the 1800's the wonders of the natural world were seen as proof of God, and studying nature was an act of religious devotion. Then new theories about geology and fossils fueled speculation that the earth was older than the Bible claimed. Ideas about evolution—which were not new-gained prominence. Marx and Engels wrote *The Communist Manifesto* and philosopher Friedrich Nietzsche pronounced "God is dead" in a political and social environment that attacked religion. The sciences became "professional," which meant scientists would exclude "pronouncements on origins, purposes and ultimate meanings,"[1] and divorced itself from faith.

    Maybe it's just as well, because science isn't equipped to handle some issues. The Bible touches on science, but it's not a science book and doesn't pretend to be one. It's a spiritual guide that answers questions like, "Why are we here?" "What's the purpose of life?" "How can we find hope?" "Who created the universe?" "Where did life come from?" and other profound questions science can't answer.

Sometimes science slips back into commenting on "origins, purposes and ultimate meanings" but its positions are unconvincing. We're told life need only "arise on one planet in a billion billion"[2] and the odds sound reasonable until you learn scientists believe creating DNA *deliberately* is impossible.[3] Impossible means zero chance, especially if you expect it to happen randomly. Physicists believe the "Higgs Bosun" is the mechanism that enabled the Big Bang to convert energy into matter, but it's popularly called "The God Particle," as if it *is* God.[4] Replicated DNA is called synthetic DNA (synthetic: made artificially[5]), giving the impression we're able to create the building blocks of life, when all we can do is replicate them from existing DNA. The media leads us to believe science has it all figured out, but it doesn't—and won't unless it turns to faith to find the missing pieces of the puzzle.

Faith and science describe different aspects of reality. You won't find the details of photosynthesis, calculus or heart surgery in the Bible. You won't find the meaning of life, the first cause of the universe or the promise of hope and spiritual fulfillment in a science book. We need both science and faith to give us the whole picture.

When we understand this, our sense of awe is put in its rightful place and, instead of congratulating ourselves for unraveling the mysteries of creation, we acknowledge the infinite genius that created it.

26

Miracles

Charlton Heston may have parted the waters of the Red Sea in the movies, but it's irrational to believe this actually happened. How can anyone think it did?

Scuba diving is so commonplace it's easy to overlook its complexity. Divers need specialized protection, life support, and education to survive in a truly hostile environment. Wet suits keep the body warm, preventing hypothermia; masks enable vision while allowing the purging of water and pressure equalization; pressurized cylinders carry air; regulators convert the air to breathable pressure; fins enhance propulsion; weight belts compensate for the weight of the equipment and the body's buoyancy to achieve weightlessness.

Divers must follow rules. Decompression charts dictate the maximum "bottom time" to avoid bends. Pressure in the ears must be equalized with changes in depth to prevent ruptured eardrums. When ascending, the breath must not be held because expanding high pressure air will explode the lungs. Deep diving can cause nitrogen narcosis, impairing mental acuity and causing irrational, dangerous behavior. Disobey the rules and the consequences are severe.

Man has mastered natural laws and enabled himself to safely swim with the fishes. This would have been considered improbable, and even miraculous, not very long ago.

There are lots of improbable miracles in the Bible. Some are from the Old Testament, like God's sending plagues on Egypt,[1] convincing Pharaoh to release the Hebrews,[2] parting the Red Sea to allow them to escape,[3] and raining down bread ("manna from heaven")[4] that kept the tribe from starving afterward.

The plagues were astonishing. God changed the Nile River into blood,[5] sent locusts that devoured everything,[6] covered the land with frogs,[7] and killed the firstborn of every house.[8] The selectivity of the plagues makes them even more amazing. Even though they lived among the Egyptians, the Hebrews were spared.[9]

In the New Testament, Jesus performed many miracles. He raised the dead,[10] turned water into wine,[11] made blind men see,[12] fed five thousand people with two fish and five loaves of bread,[13] walked on water,[14] calmed a storm[15] and healed a number of sick and crippled people.[16, 17] After his resurrection, Jesus met Saul of Tarsus, a leading persecutor of Christianity, and converted him into its leading advocate.[18] Christ's miracles lack the grand scale of those in the Old Testament, and they're performed on a more personal level. They're also acts of love rather than punishment. They demonstrate God's change from a disciplinarian trying to coax one stubborn nation to live by his laws[19] to a compassionate God offering love and eternal life to all people.[20]

There are at least three ways to look at miracles. First, there are skeptics who believe the miracles aren't actual events but are legends that were made up to press political and sociological issues. According to DePaul University Professor John Dominic Crossan, the "Gospels are parables about power and authority" in "an occupied country with a lot of poverty, malnutrition and sickness. Jesus was "healing" people ideologically, saying the Kingdom of God is against this system." Others say "the resurrection never happened, because accounts of Christ's rising are meant metaphorically, and that "one robs the Bible of its richness and poetry by insisting it should be read literally."[21]

Second, some skeptics believe the events happened but that there is a naturalistic explanation for them. For example, some "search for evidence of a volcanic eruption that could have caused the Red Sea to part" and theorize about a comet that "swept across the Bethlehem skies, disguised as a Star in the East.[22]

They also suggest explanations for some of Jesus' miracles. The healing miracles are attributed to psychosomatic illness, spontaneous remission or deliberate deception. Catalepsy, an hysterical self-induced trance that leaves a person motionless, has been suggested as the basis for the raising from the dead.[23] For miracles that aren't as readily explainable, like the feeding of the five thousand or the calming of the storm, skeptics reply that the events aren't mentioned anywhere besides the Bible and can't be accepted without other substantiation.[24]

Corroboration can be difficult to find, since a comprehensive non-biblical historical record of ancient times doesn't exist. But archaeological evidence often confirms accounts of biblical events and personages and, as more discoveries are made, the accuracy of the Bible is increasingly supported.[25] It's used as a guide by archaeologists and is regarded as essential to understanding the contexts of their findings.[26] The Bible also exceeds the standards by which historians determine the reliability of ancient writings.[27]

This brings us to the third approach to miracles. Many Christians combine historical facts with the extraordinary change they've experienced within themselves, and find that it's not much of a stretch to believe in Christ's works. These people believe that the miracles literally happened.

We only need to look around to find everyday man-made miracles. It's amazing how many things we can do today that were once considered impossible. We fly, send men to the moon, wipe out smallpox, transmit television images, communicate on the internet, practice anesthesia, and do hundreds of things every day through the miracle of electricity. Holographic images amaze our senses (anyone who's been on the Twilight Zone Tower of Terror ride at Disney World can't help but be fascinated by the realistic ghostly images). These things have come to pass as the result of accelerating technical development in all fields. One certainty about the future is that man will continue to perform ever more miracles himself.

If mankind can do all this by manipulating natural laws, why is it so difficult to believe that God can perform miracles by manipulating the universe he created? Is it because they defy logic? Interestingly, even the natural world is beyond reason until scientists have experimented enough to figure out how it works.

That's why the scientific method exists. Its purpose is to discover through trial and error those things that can't be learned through logic alone. The scientific method consists of six steps:

1. State the problem.
2. Form a hypothesis (using logic to express a possible explanation).
3. Test the hypothesis by experimenting and observing.
4. Collect data from Step 3.
5. Analyze and interpret data from Step 4.
6. Draw conclusions and either validate or modify the hypothesis.[28]

If logic alone could explain everything, the scientific method would stop at Step 2. It doesn't, because nature doesn't always act the way man expects it will. In other words, thinking alone without experimentation can't explain the physical world.

Philosopher, scholar and Christian C.S. Lewis defined a miracle as "an interference with nature by a supernatural power,"[29] which puts them beyond the scope of science. Supernatural events aren't repeatable or testable, so the scientific method is fatally impaired as a device used to understand them.

The inability to experiment and test hypotheses cripples logic in the effort to explain miraculous events. It falls short in explaining them just as it would fall short in explaining the physical world if the scientific method wasn't available. A different tool, beyond the scientific method, is needed to make sense of miracles: this tool is faith. Reason without the scientific method can't explain the physical universe. Reason without spiritual faith can't explain miracles.

Those who have faith *can* explain them. When a person has faith, his perception is expanded to include the spiritual and miracles—especially when the individual has experienced them personally—aren't so unbelievable after all.

The central event in Christianity is a miracle, and it's a miracle that makes walking on water look easy. Jesus was nailed to a cross, rose from the dead,[30] and appeared to humans. And not just a few men. He was seen by the women at the tomb,[31] the eleven remaining disciples,[32] a crowd of five hundred[33] and others. The reactions of these observers are perhaps the greatest proofs of the resurrection. Anyone seeing the risen Christ would be sure to tell others what he had seen, and word of it would have become general knowledge. This may be the reason the story of Christ spread as quickly and widely as it did, despite the opposition of the authorities. Most telling is the behavior of the disciples, who were commanded by a risen Christ to go out into the world to baptize believers and teach the word.[34] Just days earlier, one disciple betrayed him,[35] one disowned him[36] and the rest lost their faith in him.[37] Then, after seeing and speaking to him, they did as he directed with a fervor that cost them their lives.[38] Unless the resurrection really happened, why did the apostles elect to pursue lives culminating in violent death, instead of resuming the occupations they had left just three years earlier?

Given the evidence, the greatest miracle of all is believable.

The miracle of the resurrection overshadows all of the others. One Saturday morning in our Bible study, the discussion turned to miracles like the one about Jonah living for three days inside a fish.[39] An orthopedic surgeon in the group put it well when he said, "If you believe in the resurrection, then believing that a man spent three days in the belly of a fish is no big deal."

Great point. The resurrection makes all the other miracles look easy. (Come to think of it, maybe Jonah's feat *is* easy. I'll bet that man, with today's technology, could figure out how to enable a man to survive inside a fish for three days!)

It can be hard to believe in miracles. They're certainly difficult to believe when you're operating from a solely secular, logical point of view. That's because secularity and logic limit our thought processes to nonspiritual experiences. Once I became a believer, my experiences were expanded to include God, something that was previously absent. My personal relationship with Christ and its impact on me is a huge miracle, and one that I know is real. It supports the plausibility of all the other miracles.

No less an authority than Billy Graham has stated that belief in most miracles isn't necessary for salvation.[40] Except for the resurrection,[41] it's not necessary to believe in them to be a Christian. Personally, I didn't pay much attention to them until I had faith. This was just as well, because without faith to provide perspective, miracles are stumbling stones for logical people.

Jesus used miracles as signs of his divinity that couldn't be ignored or dismissed. Today, we can see them in the same way and use them to help bring us to his message.

27

Other Religions and Belief Systems

Will the One True Religion please stand up?

✥✥✥✥✥✥✥✥✥✥✥

Buddhism, Shintoism, Baha'i, Islam, Mormonism, Judaism, Christian Science, Scientology, New Age, Hinduism, Taoism, Spiritualism, Voodoo, Wicca, Astrology, Shamanism, Animism, Kabbalah, Sikhism, Jainism, Cao Dai, Tenrikyo, Zoroastrianism, Native American religions, Revivalist Hellenic Polytheism, Maori, Unitarian-Universalism, Neo-Paganism, Juche, Rastafarianism, Sufism…and on…and on…and on. This is a sampling of the world's current belief systems and doesn't include those that existed in the past, only to disappear.

The beliefs are incredibly diverse. Islam is based on revelations given to the Prophet Mohammed from God by the Angel Gabriel. Mohammed is said to be the last, and greatest, prophet in a line that includes Abraham, Moses and Jesus.[1] Buddhists don't worship any gods, but believe they are caught in a repetitive cycle of rebirth and suffering during which they attempt to relinquish selfish desires. The ultimate goal—Nirvana—is reached through "the blowing out" of the "flame of desire."[2] Hindus believe in continuous reincarnation but also worship one God whose individual characteristics are represented by a pantheon of lesser gods.[3] Scientology professes that man is immortal and claims believers can "accomplish (their) goals, gain lasting happiness (and) achieve new, higher states of awareness and ability" by using its system.[4] New Age is an umbrella term covering a wide range of beliefs from which individual adherents select their own personal preferences. A common belief is that "God" is a name for the energy that interconnects everything in the universe. New Agers compose their individual belief systems from a potpourri that includes spirit channeling, vegetarianism, astrology, holistic medicine, UFO's, numerology, and mystical quartz crystals among others.[5]

All of them attract followers. Why is this? It's because man has a need to come to terms with the spiritual presence he intuitively senses exists.

Christianity provides spiritual support for believers. But the others provide spiritual support for billions of people, too. What is it about Christ that convinces us that he's the real thing? First, we have the confirmed historical fulfillment of prophecies. The Old Testament predicted and described the coming of Christ in numerous passages written hundreds and even thousands of years before he came to earth and fulfilled them.

Second, archeological evidence validates the Bible.

Third, and most importantly, Jesus proved his godliness when he rose from the dead and energized his dejected followers to create a dynamic religion that eventually spread the messages of peace, love and hope across the planet. And since Christ's deity was proven by the resurrection, Christianity is imbued with credibility.

The religions of the world can be neatly divided into two groups. One group consists of those that believe man must earn his way into heaven based on his works.[6] The other group believes man can achieve his place in heaven through grace from God and that good works will follow as a consequence of faith. The second group is pretty exclusive since it only has one member: Christianity. Christians are able to live as the imperfect beings we are with the knowledge that our sins are forgiven even though we sometimes fall short of God's standards. Members of other religions are also in a struggle with sin but must live with uncertainty about their fate in the afterlife.

All people, regardless of faith, are prone to sin. God knows this and knows that if we have faith our behavior will improve, even if we fail at times. His grace is evident in his allowing us to seek forgiveness and then move on, knowing that our afterlife is secure. This is far superior to other faiths that require man to keep an eye on his moral abacus, constantly guessing whether the beads on the good side outweigh those on the bad side, and wondering where he'll go in the afterlife.

Deep in our souls we know there is a power beyond our understanding. Isn't it important to know who this power is and what he thinks? Wouldn't it be worthwhile to listen to him if he came to talk with us? This is just what happened in the person of Jesus Christ. God came to earth in a human body, lived among us, spoke to us, and left us with the Word of God. This direct contact with God, and the grace he offers, is what sets Christianity apart from the others.

28

The Jews

The Jewish people have been persecuted for centuries. How could Christians develop the poisonous mindset that caused this? What is the Christian view of the Hebrews?

✣✣✣✣✣✣✣✣✣✣✣

Jesus stood before the governor, Pontius Pilate,[1] accused of the capital crime of blasphemy for calling himself God.[2] Despite Pilate's insistence that he can find no basis for execution, a crowd including the chief priests, the rulers and the people[3] is unyielding and shouting "Crucify him! Crucify him!"[4] Finally, Pilate relents.[5]

He's flogged and then left with a company of soldiers. They strip him, dress him in a scarlet robe, twist together a crown of thorns, place it on his head and put a staff in his hand. Kneeling before him, they mock him as "king of the Jews." He is spit upon and the soldiers repeatedly strike him on the head with the staff. Then he's dressed back in his clothes and led away to be crucified.[6]

He carries his cross to Golgotha, the "Place of the Skull," where he is nailed to it between two others.[7] His clothes are taken and divided by casting lots.[8] Passersby, the chief priests, teachers of the law, the elders[9] and even the criminals he's crucified with hurl insults at him.[10] "Save yourself! Come down from the cross, if you are the Son of God!"[11] "Let him come down now from the cross, and we will believe in him."[12] "Aren't you the Christ? Save yourself and us!"[13]

Finally, he cries out and dies.[14] A soldier pierces his side with a spear to verify his demise, and determines that the order to break his legs to hasten death needn't be followed.[15]

For centuries, artists have graphically displayed the crucifixion of Christ by the Romans and the involvement of the Jewish hierarchy in it. Two thousand years later, the event continues to raise passions among both Christians and Jews. For Christians, the emotion is awe at the suffering Jesus endured in sacrificing himself to atone for their personal sins.[16] Jews are focused on the portrayal of the role their ancestors played, and are concerned that it inflames anti-Semitism.[17]

There are reasons the groups see the event so differently. One is that believers see the execution as the fulfillment of Old Testament prophecies.[18,19] Christians believe that Jesus was the messiah, the king and deliverer of the Jews, whose being despised and rejected was predicted in ancient prophecy.[20] In being crucified, prophecies of the Old Testament[21] and Christ himself[22] were realized. In order for Jesus to be confirmed as the messiah, this event had to happen.[23]

In this context, Christians see Jews as acting at God's behest. It's reminiscent of God's inflicting the ten plagues on Egypt, so that the Hebrews could hand down the account of his miracles to their descendants. Despite Pharaoh's willingness to relent and release the Hebrews, God "hardened (Pharaoh's) heart" to justify the completion of the plagues.[24] Just as Pharaoh was made to act in a way he didn't choose, so the Hebrews at the time of the crucifixion were players in a scene in which the outcome was determined by God. For this reason, neither individual Jews nor the Jewish people at large deserve malice for Jesus' execution.

Christians believe Christ was the sacrifice that atoned for each individual person's sins.[25] Blame for his death is put squarely on our shoulders as individuals and not on any third party, including the Jewish people.[26] Most Jews probably have as much familiarity with the New Testament as most Christians have of the Koran. This may foster the impression that Christianity condemns Judaism for the crucifixion while, in reality, Christians see themselves as the perpetrators.

Nonetheless, antipathy between Jews and Christians began in the First Century. Early Christians, who were Jews themselves, had a mission to convert others. This gave rise to Christian Jews[27] "who remained a group within Judaism."[28] But the dynamic changed as Gentiles (non-Jews) were converted. The Gentiles saw no point in observing Jewish customs (as Jewish converts did), weren't inclined to recognize their faith's Jewish underpinnings, and came to the view that "Rome's destruction of Jerusalem in A.D. 70 was nothing but the merited judgement of providence for the murder of Jesus."[29]

After an unsuccessful revolt against the Romans, in A.D. 135, the Jews were exiled, extinguishing the ancient state of Israel and beginning nearly 2000 years of dispersion.[30] Living in foreign lands, the Jewish people were insular and refused to assimilate into the local cultures. In difficult times, this made them a perennial scapegoat for the surrounding populations.[31]

Eventually, in the Middle Ages, resentment of the Jews became lethal. The general population exploded and economic changes were made that barred Jews from many occupations. The feudal system required a Christian oath in order to farm and Christian guilds were formed that controlled employment. In the end, the Jews were left with limited opportunities.[32] Since the church had "stigmatized lending money at interest,"[33] banking and money lending were among few activities open to them. Unfortunately, their participation in finance would come to further exacerbate anti-Semitism.

Hatreds stemming from charges of usury and deicide (the killing of Jesus) fomented the murder of Jews by mobs,[34] and promoted the creation of damning myths. Christians believed Jews killed Christians for blood needed for Satanic rituals and that they spread the Black Plague by poisoning wells. In Passion Plays they were "depicted as demons who knew full well that Christ was the Son of God." It was also believed that the Jews had literally stabbed Christ.[35,36] In short, Jews were seen as the embodiment of evil.

This hatred is not justified by scripture, but has historically been incited by economic factors. The notion that Jews are to be detested because "they killed Christ" is a weak excuse that sanctioned persecution of Jews for what sounds like a higher and even justifiable reason. As wrong-headed as it is, there are people who still harbor this grudge as well as economic resentment, and Jews are acutely aware of it.

Like the Inquisitions and the Crusades—which had strong anti-Semitic strains within them—anti-Semitism is the product of institutions operating under the banner of Christianity while committing acts and promoting doctrines contrary to the teachings of Christ. The success the church had in doing this has left an ugly legacy: there are Christians who have misgivings about the Jews, and there are Jews who mistrust Christians.

This is troublesome because of who the Jews are: the chosen people of God.[37] They are the precursor to Christianity; without the Hebrews the Christian faith wouldn't exist.[38] Over thousands of years, God has had his hands full with his "stiff-necked people." He called them this because of their stubbornness and repeated refusal to obey his commands.[39] Their failure to accept Jesus as messiah was another of these defiant episodes, and it culminated in salvation being offered to the Gentiles in addition to the Hebrews to whom Jesus originally preached.[40]

God hasn't given up on his chosen people. As individuals they are free to come to Christ at any time and be saved. And, if the Book of Revelation is read literally, as a nation they will be able to come to God in the end times and then be saved.[41]

It's apparent that the Jewish people are special in God's eyes. They're a very small portion of the world's population—13 million out of 6 billion, or .002%[42]—and are dispersed throughout the world. Despite this, they've been able to maintain their homogeneity as a religion and culture.

They contribute to society with works out of all proportion to their number: science, law, medicine and other professions are all richer because of their participation. Social causes, foundations and, ultimately, all of mankind, benefit from them.

Israel is a tiny country, about the size of New Jersey, with limited natural resources and no oil. The absence of oil in a petroleum rich region has generated the observation that "when

Moses led the Hebrews out of Egypt he should have taken a right instead of a left."[43] It's a focal point of the world, with an array of enemies on its doorstep who have threatened, bombed, attacked and terrorized it for decades. The toughness, resilience and dedication of its people commands respect, often grudgingly, from the rest of the world.

Christian literalists believe that the Jewish return to Israel after almost two thousand years is an event that presages the second coming of Christ.[44] Others believe that the end times descriptions were written "to stiffen the resolve in the early Christian movement to withstand persecution by the Roman Empire" and that they "hold little meaning for Christians today,"[45] so Israel's current state is irrelevant.

Either way, the Jewish people deserve the support and respect of the Christian community. Judaism can explain its existence without Christianity, but Christianity can't explain its existence without Judaism. As one pastor puts it, "The Jewish people gave the world Abraham, Isaac, Jacob, and the prophets, of whom there was "not a Baptist in the bunch."[46] Jesus was Jewish, and his teachings are based on Judaic morals, ethics, history and Yahweh, the Hebrew God.

Jews and Christians worship the same God and their histories and futures are inextricably intertwined. Both should recognize that animosity between them is misguided, especially since the Jewish people have been, and will continue to be, central players in the story of Christianity.

29

Elvis Has Left the Building[1] ...or Has He?

After all the stumbling stones have been hurdled, there can still be questions. In the end, there is only one indisputable proof of God.

> And I may be obliged to defend
> Every love, every ending
> Or maybe there's no obligations now
> Maybe there's a reason to believe
> We all will be received
> In Graceland.
>
> —*"Graceland," by Paul Simon*[2] —

A lawyer friend once expressed his skepticism about Christ by recounting a meeting he had with new clients. While engaging in small talk, he told them of a trip he was taking to Memphis, Tennessee, and jokingly remarked he was going there to find Elvis

Presley. His clients were aghast at his attempt at humor because they both believed Elvis was still alive.

Despite the witnesses, autopsy reports, and media attention given to the demise of a cultural icon, people still believe a dead man is alive. My friend's point was that if this can happen today, it's easy to see the same phenomenon happening with the story of Christ, in a time when neither forensic science nor mass media even existed.

The two cases are fundamentally different. With Elvis, the evidence points to his demise, and theories have sprung up to explain his continued life. With Christ, the evidence supports his resurrection, while theories have been contrived to argue that he didn't rise from the dead.

Skeptics have constructed various scenarios to debunk the resurrection. The "swoon" theory postulates that Jesus had fainted or been drugged. Thinking he was dead, the Romans took him down from the cross and turned him over to be buried. In the coolness of the tomb Christ is said to have recovered and then lived out his life in India.[3]

The "theft" theory proposes that the followers of Jesus stole his body from the grave.[4] They then invented tales of his after-death appearances to promote a faith they knew to be fraudulent. Neither theory is plausible but explaining them here would miss the point, which is that people will believe what they want regardless of the evidence.

Despite the study by historians, digging by archeologists, thinking by philosophers and analyses by theologians for two thousand years, only one indisputable proof of the truth of Christ exists. This proof is the change that happens within people when they come to faith. Sometimes the change is obvious to others: an addict overcomes his addiction; a violent and argumentative person becomes peaceful. With others, it's a solace that enables them to live with an inner peace and strength.

Elvis may or may not have left the building. Either way, he doesn't have the capacity to change people's lives. Every believer can attest that Jesus does. It takes faith to get to this point, but once a person believes in Christ, the indisputable proof of his power resides within the individual himself. It's at this point, when the believer personally experiences a relationship with Christ, and he knows a miracle has happened within him, that the stumbling stones vanish.

30

A Final Point to Ponder

"Just because you don't believe it doesn't mean it isn't true."

—*Actor Dennis Franz, playing Nathaniel Messinger, in the 1998 movie "City of Angels"*

Afterword

After overcoming the stumbling stones, what's next?

The best way to know the reality of Jesus Christ is to open your mind and give him a chance. Sincere faith brings changes in a person that are remarkable because they're positive, undeniable and occur through no effort on the believer's part. These changes cause Christians to become even more convicted because they know God has actively interceded in their lives and demonstrated his ability and willingness to develop a personal relationship with them.

Coming to Christ is an intensely personal act in which you accept that Jesus died to atone for your sins. When you accept him, he washes you of your sins, makes you perfect in God's eyes, and assures you of a place in heaven.

No formal ceremony, or even the presence of others, is required. A silent prayer in solitude is an effective, appropriate way to begin a personal relationship with Jesus.[1] As communication through prayer becomes a regular habit you'll probably find that problems get solved more readily and it's easier to live with those that don't get solved at all.

The promise of eternity doesn't come with strings attached. It's a gift from God. You're not obligated to "give your life to Jesus," forsake your non-Christian friends or even swear off smoking, cursing and drinking. But it's entirely possible that as you learn more and spend more time with Christians you'll find subtle changes taking place.

If you've really opened your mind, it's important to nurture your faith by learning about it and exposing yourself to knowledgeable, mature Christians who can share the importance of their beliefs just by being themselves. It's almost as if they spread faith in Christ by osmosis. Attending the right church can provide these contacts along with structured educational opportunities and friendship with other Christians who are in various stages of faith. Sometimes, when we hit rough spots in life, it's helpful just to be at church to soak up the positivity that Christians exude. It's contagious and helps to recharge your spiritual batteries after spending time in life's trenches.

Christian faith puts our lives in the perspective of eternity and in doing so takes the sting out of death. It also gives us the strength of knowing that God is willing to listen and provide the guidance that comes with a prayerful examination of our problems and fears.

Christianity empowers the believer to negotiate life with peace and confidence. And it enables him to answer the question "What will happen to you if you die today?" happily with "I'll be in heaven with Jesus."

If you sincerely come to faith, this is what's next for you.

Acknowledgments

Many people contributed to my coming to faith, knowingly or not. By extension, they also helped write this book. Some provided insights during classes, discussions and conversations, others spoke through their deeds, and many just provided good examples by being what they are: committed Christians.

Interacting with knowledgeable believers, and watching them deal with life's difficulties, brought the strength of God home to me. Meg Foss, an elderly lady who was beset by osteoporosis and got around with a walker, always had the same response when asked how she was: she'd smile sweetly and say "I'm blessed." Ken Brooks, a retired industrial engineer, helped operate a rescue mission for the indigent for many years before concern about the homeless became fashionable. Some members participated in a community outreach program called "Celebrate Recovery" to help people find "freedom from hurts, habits and hangups." This program, offered free of charge by First Central, is so successful that secular agencies refer clients to it. In sickness or times of bereavement, the congregation can be counted on to pray, send cards, visit, or offer kind words.

Most remarkable is the attitude they have: positive and forward-looking despite current pain or sadness. Surrounded by such people, faith is contagious.

Certain people had active roles in opening my mind and developing my faith. Members of the Saturday morning Bible study group discussed a wide variety of issues and brought understanding to each. The members were from many walks of life: UPS driver, physician, fireman, jet mechanic, surgeon, architect, electric company lineman, teacher, college professor and others. At various times, the group included Chris Ames, Dan Appleton, Sean Brennan, Bill Chenaille, Jim Farley, Tim Galas, Woody Geoffroy, Pete Goodreau, Kurt Larsen, Richard Sanders, Lloyd Smith, Paul Titus and Ken Williams. Tom Russell, with his wit, knowledge, and practical point of view, was especially helpful.

The "Christianity 101" class I attended early on was taught by Pastor Doug Gray. His effervescent, sincere faith, and entertaining teaching style helped stoke my desire to learn more.

Dr. David Ballan is the subject of Chapter 2. I'd probably still be skeptical of Christianity if it weren't for his interest in bringing me to faith.

Pastor Robert Riedy, Senior Pastor at First Central Baptist Church, is a gifted preacher whose down to earth, dynamic sermons teach about the wonders of God each week. Bob was generous with his time in discussing issues of faith with me and offering support in the writing of this book.

J. Noyes was a source of encouragement and was generous in sharing his knowledge of the publishing business.

Joe Martin was the de facto leader of the Saturday morning Bible study. Understanding that I was a skeptic, he and the rest of the group welcomed me and addressed many of the issues that stood between me and faith. Whether through the Bible study group, Sunday School teaching, private conversations, or dinners that we enjoyed with our wives, he was a consistent source of encouragement and information. Without Joe's faith and knowledge to draw on, this book couldn't have been written.

Notes

Unless noted otherwise, Bible references are from the Life Application Study Bible, New International Version published jointly by Tyndale House Publishers, Inc., Wheaton, IL and Zondervan Publishing House, Grand Rapids, MI. Copyrights 1988, 1989, 1991.

Chapter 1
1. 1 Corinthians 15:54-55

Chapter 2
1. Romans 9:31-33
2. 1 Corinthians 1:22-23

Chapter 3
1. Jim Morrison, The Soft Parade. From the album "The Soft Parade." Elektra Records. 1969

Chapter 4
1. Luke 1:34-35
2. John 19:18
3. Luke 24:20-24
4. John 11:38-44
5. Mark 1:34
6. John 6:19
7. Matthew 4:2
8. NIV Note for Mark 2:10, p. 1729
9. Mark 14:61-64
10. Luke 22:56-60
11. Luke 24:37-39

[12] Acts 5:12-14

[13] Foxe, John, *Christian Martyrs of the World*, prepared by W. Grinton Berry, (Grand Rapids, MI, Baker Book House Company, 1998) pp. 6-13

[14] McDowell, Josh, *More Than a Carpenter* (Wheaton, IL: Tyndale House Publishers, 1977) p. 103

[15] Messiah. 11/29/07. *http://www.woodgord.redbridge.sch.uk/rs/year7/lentmessiah.html*

[16] McDowell, Josh, *More Than a Carpenter* (Wheaton, IL: Tyndale House Publishers, 1977) p. 103

[17] McDowell, Josh, *A Ready Defense* (Nashville, TN: Thomas Nelson, Inc. 1993) p. 211

[18] Ibid., p. 212

[19] Strobel, Lee, *The Case for Christ* (Grand Rapids, MI: Zondervan, 1998) p. 200

[20] McDowell, Josh, *A Ready Defense* (Nashville, TN: Thomas Nelson, Inc. 1993) p. 212

[21] Ibid., p. 213

Chapter 5

[1] Rogers, Dale Evans, "God Is Prayer." *The Power of Prayer*, edited by Dale Salwak (New York: MJF Books, 1998) p. 51

[2] Psalms 139:13-16

[3] Psalms 139:23-24

[4] Philippians 4:6

[5] Philippians 4:7

[6] Nouwen, Henri j.m., "The Paradox of Prayer," *The Power of Prayer*, edited by Dale Salwak (NewYork: MJF Books, 1998) p. 46

[7] Williamson, Marianne, "Ladders to God," *The Power of Prayer*, edited by Dale Salwak (New York: MJF Books, 1998)p

[8] Miller, Samuel h., "Prayer and Life," *The Power of Prayer*, edited by Dale Salwak (New York: MJF Books, 1998) p. 91

Chapter 6

1. 1 John 1:9
2. Acts 3:19
3. Forgiving and Repenting. 5/2/2008. *http://www.churchtriumphant.com/forgiving_repenting_2.htm*
4. Acts 2:38
5. Colossians 3:13
6. Ephesians 4:31-32
7. 2 John 11:6
8. Romans 12:18
9. Titus 3:10
10. Luke 17:3
11. Matthew 18:15-17
12. Romans 13:3-4
13. Romans 2:16

Chapter 7

1. *NIV Compact Dictionary of the Bible* (Grand Rapids, MI: Zondervan Publishing House. 1989) p. 498
2. Exodus 12:29
3. Exodus 12:7
4. Exodus 12:13
5. Exodus 12:25-27
6. Isaiah 1:15-16
7. Leviticus 1:4
8. Matthew 6:4
9. Numbers 23:1-2
10. Numbers 22:40
11. NIV Note for Leviticus 20:1-3, p. 197
12. Judges 3:7
13. Leviticus 5:17-19

14. Leviticus 4:3
15. Leviticus 4:23
16. Leviticus 5:7
17. Leviticus 5:5-13
18. John 1:29
19. 1 John 1:9
20. 1 Thessalonians 5:9-10
21. Matthew 6:10
    Matthew 7:12

Chapter 8
1. Distel, Barbara, *Dachau Concentration Camp* (Comite International de Dachau, 1972)
2. *The American Heritage Dictionary of the English Language* (New York: Dell Publishing, 1979)
3. Matthew 4:1-9
4. Comparison of Christian Denominations - Beliefs (Part 1) 5/5/2008. *http://christianity.about.com/od/denominationscomparison/ss/comparebeliefs1_7.htm*
5. William Willimon, Satan: A Second Look. 6/8/2007. *http://www.chapel.duke.edu/worship/sunday/viewsermon.aspx?id=18*
6. Galatians 5:20-21
7. Exodus 20:14
8. 2 Corinthians 5:10
9. Thomas Sowell, "Non-Judgmental" Nonsense. 5/5/2008. *http://jewishworldreview.com/cols/sowell031208.php3*
10. Jeffery l. Sheler, Hell Hath No Fury. 4/23/2008. *http://www.italianstudies.org/hui235/U_S_%20Modern%20thinking%20says%2*, p.3
11. Matthew 25:46
12. Revelation 20:11-15
13. Romans 12:19

[14] Inferno-Dante Alighieri, 2/26/04. Barnes and Noble Learning Network. *http://www.sparknotes.com/poetry/inferno/summary.html*

[15] Foote, Timothy and the Editors of Time-Life Books, *The World of Bruegel c.1525-1569* (New York: Time-Life Books, 1972) p. 63, pp. 66-67

[16] Jeffery l. Sheler, Hell Hath No Fury. 4/23/2008. *http://www.italianstudies.org/hui235/U_S_%20Modern%20thinking%20says%2, p.2*

[17] Ibid., p. 6

[18] Ibid., p. 7

[19] Ibid., p. 6

[20] Andrew Delbanco, The Death of Satan. 2/18/2006. *http://www.washingtonpost.com/wp-srv/style/longterm/books/chap1/deathof.htm*

[21] Romans 10:9

Chapter 9

[1] *NIV Compact Dictionary of the Bible* (Grand Rapids, MI: Zondervan Publishing House, 1989) p. 556

[2] Nehemiah 9-Israel Confesses Their Sin. 12/4/2007. *http://www.enduringword.com/commentaries/1609.htm pp.1-2*

[3] Exodus 20:12-17

[4] Galatians 5:19-21

[5] Galatians 5:22

[6] Matthew 22:39

[7] 2 Thessalonians 3:11-12

[8] 1 Peter 4:8-10

[9] Romans 2:1

[10] Acts 26:12-19

[11] Colossians 4:3

[12] Acts 16:23

[13] 2 Corinthians 11:25

[14] Romans 7:19

[15] Romans 7:21-23

Chapter 10 (continued footnotes)

16. Romans 12:10
17. Romans 12:20

Chapter 10

1. Luke 23:42-43
2. Case of Carla Faye Tucker. 2/15/2004. *http://mitglied.lycos.de/PeterWill/penal7.htm*
3. Tucker Dies By Lethal Injection. 2/15/2004. *http://www.cnn.com/US/9802/03/tucker.executed/index.html*
4. 1 John 1:9
5. Romans 13: 1-5
6. 1 Corinthians 4:3-5
7. Romans 3:21-24
8. 2 Corinthians 5:10
9. NIV Note for Matthew 16:27, p. 1686

Chapter 11

1. The Holy Trinity. 3/17/2004. *www.sundayschoollessons.com/trin.html*
2. Genesis 1:1-31
3. What Do Baptists Believe? 3/17/2004. *http://baptistnsw.asn.au/about/faith*
4. Acts 2:22
5. 1 Peter 2:22
6. NIV Note for Matthew 27:46, p. 1718
7. John 15:11
8. John 2:14-16
9. Genesis 1:2
10. Judges 14:6
11. 1 Samuel 10:9-10
12. Romans 8:9
13. Romans 9:1

Chapter 12

1. Kushner, Harold S., *When Bad Things Happen to Good People* (New York, Schocken Books: 1981) p. 29
2. Ibid., p. 134
3. Genesis 1:28-30
4. Matthew 22:37
5. Lewis, c.s., *Mere Christianity* (San Francisco, HarperSanFrancisco, 2001) pp. 47-48
6. Fame and Infamy Surround Anna Nicole Smith. 2/12/2006. *http://abcnews.go.com/Primetime/story?id=1320909*
7. 1 Peter 4:12-14
8. Robert DeNiro. The Actors Studio, Production Code 410. Bravo Network, 1/31/99

Chapter 13

1. Simon Rees. The Christmas Truce. 6/14/2005. *http://www.firstworldwar.com/features/christmastruce.htm*
2. Matthew 5:44
3. Romans 12:20
4. 2 Corinthians 10:4
5. Romans 13:9
6. Romans 12:19
7. 1 Peter 2:23
8. Luke 22:50-51
9. Matthew 26:52
10. Exodus 20:13 *The Holy Bible, Authorized King James Version* (Nashville, TN, Holman Bible Publishers, 1979)
11. Romans 13:1
12. Romans 13:4
13. 1 Timothy 2:1-2
14. Ecclesiastes 3:1-8

[15] Mark 13:7
[16] Luke 7:2-10
[17] Acts 10:1-48
[18] Matthew 26:52
[19] Lewis, C.S., *Mere Christianity* (San Francisco, HarperSanFrancisco, 2001) p. 118
[20] Rodger Russell. What Does the Bible Say About War? 10/16/2003. http://www.lifeway.com/lwc/article_main_page/0,1703,A%sD1524422%26M%3D150033
[21] Loconte, Joseph. "Peace Now." *The Wall Street Journal*. 11/4/2005

Chapter 14
[1] Johannes Gutenberg. 3/9/2004. *www.gutenbergdigital.de/gudi/eframes/texte/framere/bio-1.htm*
[2] An Industry Born. 3/9/2004. *www.dotprint.com/fgen/history.1htm*
[3] Best Selling Non-Fiction Book. 4/16/2004. *www.guinessworldrecords.com*
[4] 2 Timothy 3:16
[5] FAQ on the Origin of the Bible, 4/16/2004 *http://www.biblebell.org/howgothb.html*
[6] International Bible Society, When Was the Bible Written? 4/16/2004. *www.gospel.com.net/ibs/bibles/about/3.php*
[7] Patrick Zukeran, Authority of the Bible. 3/6/2004. *www.probe.org/docs/auth-bib.html*
[8] Matthew 5:40
[9] NIV Note for Exodus 22:26, p. 141
[10] NIV Note for Genesis 37:34, p. 78
[11] NIV Note for Exodus 34:13, p. 158
[12] NIV Note for Exodus 21:24-25, p. 139
[13] McDowell, Josh, *A Ready Defense* (Nashville, TN: Thomas Nelson, Inc. 1993) p. 43-45

[14] Sheler, Jeffery L, *Is The Bible True?* (HarperSanFrancisco and Zondervan Publishing, 1989) p. 95
[15] Ibid., p. 112
[16] Ibid., p. 102
[17] Ibid., p. 104
[18] Pelikan, Jaroslav, *Whose Bible Is It?* (New York, Penguin Group, 2005) pp. 13-14
[19] Dr. Dale A. Robbins, Why So Many Bible Translations?. 3/8/2004. *http://www.victorious.org/translat.htm*
[20] Lewis, C.S., *The Joyful Christian* (New York, MacMillan Publishing Co., 1977) pp. 189-196
[21] The Background of the New International Version Bible, 3/9/2004 *www.gospelcom.net/ibs/niv/background.php*
[22] Ephesians 4:31
[23] Matthew 19:24-26
[24] Genesis 1:1-31
[25] Mark 2:7
[26] Matthew 22:37
[27] Ephesians 2:4
[28] Romans 2:11
[29] 1 Timothy 1:17
[30] 2 Timothy 4:1
[31] Romans 12:19
[32] Luke 12:6-7
[33] Mark 12:31

Chapter 15

[1] Assemblies of God, 2/27/2004. *http://www.solidarityinstitute.org./faith/assemblies.asp*
[2] Baptists, 2/27/2004. *http://www.solidarityinstitute.org/faith/baptist.asp*
[3] Catholics, 2/27/2004. *http://www.solidarityinstitute.org/faith/catholic.asp*

4. United Methodists, 2/28/2004. *http://www.methodx.org/thelife/askjulian.asp?act=answer&item_id=57974*
5. Orthodox Church in America, Bible. 2/28/2004. *http://www.oca.org/pages/orth_chri/orthodox-faith/doctrine/Bible.html*
6. Ecumenical Patriarchate, 11/5/2007. *www.ec-patr.org*
7. Assemblies of God, 2/27/2004 *http://www.solidarityinstitute.org/faith/assemblies.asp*
8. Fundamental Beliefs, 8/28/2005. *http://www.adventist.org/beliefs/fundamental/index.html*
9. What is the United Church of Christ? 5/23/2007. *www.ucc.org/aboutus/whatis.htm*
10. Ecumenical Patriarchate, 11/5/2007. *www.ec-patr.org*
11. What is the United Church of Christ? 5/23/2007. *www.ucc.org/aboutus/whatis.htm*
12. The Pioneers, Origin and Organization of the AME Church, 12/7/2007. *http://www.greaterstjames.org/ame_origin.htm*
12. About Us-Our Name, 12/7/2007. *http://www.ame-church.com/about-us/*
13. Mike Ford, Should Christians Handle Snakes? 3/2/2004. *www.cgg.org/index.cfm/page/literature.articles.1207ra.htm*
14. Mark 16:16-18
15. Ted Olsen, They Shall Take Up Serpents, 3/2/2004 *www.ctlibrary.com/ch/1998/58/58h025.html*
16. The History of Jonestown, 12/7/2007. *http://www.owlnet.rice.edu/~reli291/Jonestown/Jonestown.html*
17. Shea, Suzanne Strempek, *Sundays In America* (Boston: Beacon Press, 2008) p. xi.

Chapter 16

1. Corrie Ferguson and Amy N. Grupp, Constantine Converts to Christianity, 2/12/2004. *http://campus.northpark.edu/history/WebChron/EastEurope/ConstantineConverts.Cp.html*
2. Historical Overview if the Inquisition, 2/12/04. *http://es.rice.edu/ES/humsoc/Galileo/Student_Work/Trial96/loftis/overview.html*

3. Ellerbe, Helen, *The Dark Side of Christian History*. (Orlando, FL: Morningstar and Lark, 1995) pp. 78-83
4. Jason l. Slade, The Spanish Inquisition, 2/12/2004. *www.bibletopics.com/biblestudy/64.htm*
5. The Crusades, 2/12/2004 *http://www.ucalgary.ca/appliedhistory/tutor/endmiddle/bluedot/crusades.html*
6. BBC News, Provisional IRA: War, Ceasefire, Endgame? 2/12/2007. *http://news.bbc.co.uk/hi/english/ststic/in_depth/northern_ireland/2001/provisional_ira/2000/stm*
7. Ireland – the Celtic Tiger, 2/12/2007. *http://www.workinfo.com/EconHist/ireland.htm*
8. Robert P. Ingalls, Ph.D., "Ku Klux Klan." *World Book Encyclopedia* (Chicago: World Book, Inc., 2003)
9. Zaslow, Jeffrey. "In Detroit, a Blow to 'The Fist' Touches A Sensitive Nerve." *The Wall Street Journal* 3/4/2004.
10. Trofimov, Yaroslav. "An African Music Star Uses Fame and Wealth To Help Fellow Albinos." *The Wall Street Journal*. 1/6/06

Chapter 17

1. Elton John-Bernie Taupin, Tiny Dancer. From the album "Madman Across the Water." MCA Records, Inc. 1972
2. A Biography of Marx 11/7/2007 *http://www.indepthinfo.com/communist-manifesto/karl-marx.shtml*
3. Charles Colson, "We're All Born Again Now: Exploring the Boomer Soul." 1/11/2004. *http://www.dadi.org/cc_born.htm*.
4. Darcy DeMarco, Intolerance in Christianity, 5/8/2008. *http://religiousintolerance.suite101.com/article.cfm/religious_intolerance_old_and_new*
5. Tolson, Jay. "The New Old-Time Religion." *U.S. News & World Report* 12/8/03. p. 41
6. John 3:3
7. Romans 10:9-10
8. Matthew 7:1-5
9. Romans 14:10-13

10. Colossians 2:18
11. Titus 3:5
12. John 3:16
13. Ephesians 2:8-9
14. Romans 6:3-4

Chapter 18
1. History of the First Central Baptist Church of Chicopee, Massachusetts, 11/24/05
2. Annual Report-2007, First Central Baptist Church
3. Arthur C. Brooks, The Great Divide in American Giving, 4/2/2008. The International Journal of Not-for-Profit Law. *http://www.icnl.org/knowledge/ijnl/vol9iss1/special_2.htm*
4. Matthew 6:3
5. Matthew 25:42-45
6. Ephesians 2:8-10

Chapter 19
1. Romans 6:11-14
2. Matthew 5:7
3. Matthew 5:42
4. Matthew 6:14
5. Matthew 6:19
6. Matthew 7:1
7. Matthew 15:19-20
8. Matthew 25:35-40
9. Mark 7:22
10. Colossians 2:18
11. Luke 6:27
12. Phillipians 2:14
13. 1 Thessalonians 5:18

14. Ephesians 4:32
15. Ephesians 5:4
16. 2 Corinthians 12:20
17. 2 Corinthians 6:6
18. Galatians 5:20
19. Matthew 6:25
20. Galatians 5:21
21. Romans 12:19
22. Galatians 5:23
23. Ephesians 4:31
24. Ephesians 4:32
25. Luke 10:27
26. Exodus 20:13
27. Exodus 20:15
28. Exodus 20:16

Chapter 20

1. Dominguez, Alex. "Grieving dad wins suit against church." Associated Press. *The Republican*, Springfield, MA 11/1/07
2. Matthew 22:36-40
3. 2 Peter 3:16
4. NIV Note for 2 Peter 3:15-18, p. 2271

Chapter 21

1. The Jimmy Swaggart Scandal. 3/23/2004. *www.historychannel.com/speeches/archive/speech_360.html*
2. Dominick A. Miserandino Seaman, Ann – Author of Jimmy Swaggart's Biography. 3/23/2004. *www.thecelebritycafe.com/interviews/ann_seaman.html*
3. The Jimmy Swaggart Scandal. 3/23/2004. *www.historychannel.com/speeches/archive/speech_360.html*

⁴ *The American Heritage Dictionary of the English Language* (New York: Dell Publishing, 1979)
⁵ Matthew 7:1-5
⁶ 2 Corinthians 5:1

Chapter 22

¹ perception, 12/31/2007. http://dictionary.reference.com/browse/perception
² Flew, Antony, *There Is A God: How the World's Most Notorious Atheist Changed His Mind.* (New York: Harper One, 2007) pp. 96-100
³ Dennis Overbye, Einstein Letter on God Sells for $404,000. 5/18/2008. http://www.nytimes.com/2008/05/17/science/17einsteinw.html?_r=rssnyt&emc
³ Collins, Francis S. *The Language of God* (New York: Free Press, 2006) pp. 102-104
⁴ Introduction to Cyanobacteria, 12/28/2007 http://www.ucmp.berkeley.edu/bacteria/cyanointro.html
⁵ base pair, The Free Dictionary, 12/26/2007. http://www.thefreedictionary.com/base+pair
⁶ Birgit Reinert, Strings of pearls: The genome sequence of Anabaena, 12/26/2007. http://www.genomenewsnetwork.org/articles/01_02/Anabaena.shtml
⁷ From Soup to DNA, 5/9/2008. www.evolutionofdna.com/Evolution-Of-DNA.html
⁸ Noel Clark, New Scenario For First Life On Earth, 5/9/2008. http://www.medicalnewstoday.com/articles/89690.http://www.medicalnewstoday.com/articles/89690.php
⁹ Flew, Antony *There Is A God: How the World's Most Notorious Atheist Changed His Mind.* (New York: Harper One, 2007) p. 130, 172
¹⁰ Ibid., p. 173
¹¹ Ibid., p. 131
¹² Ibid., p. 132
¹³ Ibid., p. vii

14 Ibid., pp. 75-77
15 Ibid., pp. 178-179
16 Kevin B. Korb Stage Effects to the Cartesian Theater: A Review of Daniel Dennett's Consciousness Explained 2/18/2008. http://psyche.cs.monash.edu.au/vl/psyche-1-04-korbe.htm
17 Flew, Antony *There Is A God: How the World's Most Notorious Atheist Changed His Mind*. (New York: Harper One, 2007) p. 130, 172
18 Ibid., p. 176
19 Ibid., p. 175
20 The Brights, 12/26/2007. http://www.the-brights.net/
21 Collins, Francis S. *The Language of God* (New York: The Free Press, 2006) pp. 102-104
22 Greenberg, Daniel S., *Science for Sale*, (Chicago: The University of Chicago Press, 2007) p. 11
23 Felton, Eric, "When Fad Science is Bad Science" *The Wall Street Journal*, 8/27/2010
24 Scientific Community Reacts to Report of Misconduct, 8/13/2010 http://harvardmagazine.com/harvard-in-the-news/marc-hauser-reaction
25 Nicholas Wade, Harvard Finds Scientist Guilty of Misconduct, 8/20/2008. http://www.nytimes.com/2010/08/21/education/21harvard.html
26 Randy Thornhill and Craig T. Palmer. "Why Men Rape" *The Sciences* January/February 2000 (The New York Academy of Sciences)
27 "A Controversial Book on Rape" – *CBS News Early Show*, 2/11/2009 www.cbsnews.com/2100-18564_162-151345.html
28 Jerry A. Coyne and Andrew Berry, "A theory that rape has its origin in evolutionary biology is flawed," *Nature*, Vol. 404 3/9/2000
29 Naik, Gautam. "Scientists' Elusive Goal: Reproducing Study Results," *The Wall Street Journal*, 12/2/2011
30 Collins, Francis S., *The Language of God*, (New York: Free Press, 2006) p. 4
31 David G. Hallstrom, Sr. The Act of Being Politically Correct Has Gone From The Sublime To The Ridiculous 5/10/2008 http://resourcesforattorneys.com/politicallycorrectarticle.html

Chapter 23

1. Tolkien, J.R.R., *The Lord of the Rings*. (Boston, Houghton Mifflin Company, 1965)
2. Nora Connolly. Home of Middle Earth *http://213.219.43.117/york/yolmagazine/march/39.html*
3. Ken Ham, Jonathan Sarfati, Carl Wieland. Ed. Don Batten. How About Carbon Dating? 11/4/2003. *http://www.answersingenesis.org/docs2002/carbon_dating.asp*
4. Genesis 1:1-3
5. Weister, John L. *The Genesis Connection* (Nashville, TN: Thomas Nelson Publishers, 1983) pp. 17-18
6. Chris LaRocco and Blair Rothstein. The Big Bang. 7/11/2005 *www.umich.edu/-gs265/bigbang.htm*
7. Weister, John L. *The Genesis Connection* (Nashville, TN: Thomas Nelson Publishers, 1983) p.20
8. Ibid., pp. 39-44
9. Ibid., pp. 53-59
10. Ibid., pp. 37-38
11. Ibid., p. 47
12. Genesis 1:6-8
13. Weister, John L. *The Genesis Connection* (Nashville, TN: Thomas Nelson Publishers, 1983) p. 53
14. Ibid., pp. 59-60
15. Genesis 1:9-12
16. Weister, John L. *The Genesis Connection* (Nashville, TN: Thomas Nelson Publishers, 1983) pp. 61-62
17. Ibid., pp. 77-79
18. Genesis 14-18
19. The Biblical Story of Creation of the World and Man. 12/12/2007. *http://www.orthodoxphotos.com/readings/sketches/story.shtml*
20. Weister, John l. *The Genesis Connection* (Nashville, TN: Thomas Nelson Publishers, 1983) p. 98
21. Genesis 1:20-22

[22] Weister, John L. *The Genesis Connection* (Nashville, TN: Thomas Nelson Publishers, 1983) pp.117-125

[23] Genesis 1:24-27

[24] Weister, John L. *The Genesis Connection* (Nashville, TN: Thomas Nelson Publishers, 1983) p.152

[25] Grant Hallman, Ph.d., University of Toronto. Closed Systems. 5/11/2008. *http://www.physlink.com/Education/AskExperts/ae332.cfm*

[26] Famous Scientists Who Believed in God. 12/13/2007. *http://www.godandscience.org/apologetics/sciencefaith.html*

[27] Grant Hallman, Ph.d., University of Toronto. Closed Systems. 5/11/2008. *http://www.physlink.com/Education/AskExperts/ae332.cfm*

[28] Famous Scientists Who Believed in God. 12/13/2007. *http://www.godandscience.org/apologetics/sciencefaith.html*

[29] Alan Boyle, "Questioning the Big Bang." 12/13/2007. *www.msnbc.msn.com/id/3077357/*

[30] Collins, Francis S., *The Language of God* (New York: Free Press, 2006) p. 76

Chapter 24

[1] Darwin and Evolution. 3/26/2004. *http://www.geo.cornell.edu/geology/GalapagosWWW/Darwin.html*

[2] Jean-Baptiste Lamarck. 12/13/2007. *http://www.ucmp.berkeley.edu/history/lamarck.html*

[3] Krista Gowens, Charles Darwin. 10/23/2003. *http://www.mankato.msus.edu/museum/information/biography/abcde/darwin_charles.html*

[4] Darwin and Evolution. 3/26/2004. *http://www.geo.cornell.edu/geology/GalapagosWWW/Darwin.html*

[5] Darwin, Charles. The Voyage of the Beagle, *Darwin: The Indelible Stamp*. Ed. James D. Watson (Philadelphia: Running Press Book Publishers, 2005) pp. 145-146

[6] Ibid. p. 160

[7] Ibid. p. 158

[8] Ibid. p. 252

[9] Ibid. p. 255

10. Ibid. pp. 266-268
11. Ibid. p. 256
12. Ibid., pp. 378-379
13. Ibid., pp. 402-403
14. Dawkins, Richard. *The God Delusion*, (New York: Houghton Mifflin, 2008) p. 164
15. Collins, Francis S. *The Language of God* (New York: Free Press, 2006) p. 172
16. Darwin, Charles. The Voyage of the Beagle, *Darwin: The Indelible Stamp*. Ed. James D. Watson (Philadelphia: Running Press Book Publishers, 2005) p. 348
17. Ibid. p. 440
18. Ibid. p. 491
19. Teaching About Evolution and the Nature of Science. 3/26/2004. *http://books.nap.edu/books/0309063647/html/56.html*
20. Darwin, Charles. The Voyage of the Beagle, *Darwin: The Indelible Stamp*. Ed. James D. Watson (Philadelphia: Running Press Book Publishers, 2005) p. 444
21. Adaptation.12/17/2007. *http://evolution.berkely.edu/evosite/evo101/IIIE5Adaptation.shtml*
22. Freeman, Stan. "Species may evolve faster than believed." *Union-News*, Springfield, Ma. 10/20/00
23. An Introduction to Evolution, 12/17/2007. *http://evolution.berkely.edu/evosite/evo101/IIntro.shtml*
24. Ibid., p. 1
25. "Climbing Fish," *Life Episode 4*, 9/25/2011 *www.bbc.co.uk/nature/life/Goby#p004y2h5*
26. prebiotic, 5/12/2007. *http://medical.merriam-webster.com/medical/prebiotic*
27. Sean Henahan. From Primordial Soup to the Prebiotic Beach. 10/24/2003. *http://www.accessexcellence.org/WN/NM/miller.html*
28. Darwin, Charles. The Voyage of the Beagle, *Darwin: The Indelible Stamp*. Ed. James D. Watson (Philadelphia: Running Press Book Publishers, 2005) p. 705

[29] Sharon Begley. "Searching For the God Within." *Newsweek*, 1/29/01
[30] Sharon Begley. "God & the Brain." *Newsweek*, 5/7/01
[31] Lewis, C.S., "The Poison of Subjectivism," C.S. Lewis, *Christian Reflections*. Ed. Walter Hooper. (Grand Rapids: Eerdmans, 1967) p. 77
[32] Collins, Francis S. *The Language of God* (New York: Free Press, 2006) p. 27
[33] Stephen J. Gould. Nonoverlapping Magisteria. 3/28/2004. *www.cyberbuzz.gatech.edu/kaboom/interesting/gould-magisteria.html*
[34] Punctuated Equilibrium. 3/28/2004. *www.iscid.org/encyclopedia/Punctuated_Equilibrium*
[35] Collins, Francis S. *The Language of God*, (New York: Free Press, 2006) p. 161
[36] Ibid., p. 111
[37] Ibid., pp. 200-201
[38] Ibid., p. 228
[39] Ibid., p. 209
[40] Ibid., p. 153
[41] Ibid., pp. 154-156
[42] Ibid., p. 199

Chapter 25

[1] Principe, Lawrence M., *Science and Religion*. (Chantilly, VA: The Teaching Company, 2006) p. 47
[2] Dawkins, Richard. *The God Delusion*, (New York: Houghton Mifflin, 2008) p. 166
[3] Noel Clark, New Scenario For First Life On Earth, 5/9/2008. *http://www.medicalnewstoday.com/articles/89690.php*
[4] Fried, Stephen. "The Race for the Secret of the Universe." *Parade Magazine*. 7/26/2009
[5] Synthetic, The American Heritage Science Dictionary, 2005.

Chapter 26

1. NIV The Plagues, p. 117
2. Exodus 12:31
3. Exodus 14:21-22
4. Exodus 16:4
5. Exodus 7:20
6. Exodus 10:13-15
7. Exodus 8:6
8. Exodus 12:29
9. Exodus 13:13
10. John 11:43-44
11. John 2:7-11
12. Matthew 9:27-30
13. Luke 9:12-17
14. Mark 6:45-48
15. Mark 4:37-39
16. Matthew 9:20-22
17. Luke 13:10
18. Acts 9:1-15
19. 2 Kings 17:14-20
20. Romans 1:16
21. Gibbs, Nancy. The Message of Miracles. 5/13/2008. http://www.time.com/time/printout/0,8816,133993,00.html p. 6
22. Ibid., p. 5
23. The Healing Miracles. 3/13/2004. http://www.geocities.com/paultobin/healings.html p. 1,2,15
24. Historical Validation of Miracles, 12/18/2007. http://theunbelieveratlarge.wordpress.com/2007/11/18/historical-validation-of-miracles/ p. 1
25. Sheler, Jeffery, *Is the Bible True?* (HarperSanFrancisco and Zondervan Publishing 1989)pp. 254-256
26. Ibid., pp. 120-121

27 McDowell, Josh, *A Ready Defense* (Nashville, TN: Thomas Nelson Inc. 1993) pp. 43-47
28 The Scientific Method of Problem Solving, 12/18/2007. http://www.hobart.k12.in.us/jkousen/Sci_Meth/pmethod.htm p. 1
29 Lewis, C.S., *Miracles* (San Francisco: HarperSanFrancisco, 2001) p. 5
30 Mark 16:6
31 Matthew 28:8
32 Mark 16:4
33 Matthew 28:16
34 1 Corinthians 15:6
35 Mark 16:15
36 Mark 14:44-45
37 Mark 14:66-72
38 Mark 16:14
39 Foxe, John, *Foxe's Christian Martyrs of the World*, prepared by W. Grinton Berry, (Grand Rapids, MI: Zondervan, 1998) pp. 6-13
40 Jonah 1:17
41 Gibbs, Nancy. The Message of Miracles. 5/13/2008. http://www.time.com/time/printout/0,8816,133993,00.html
42 Jonah 3:14-16

Chapter 27

1 McDowell, Josh, *A Ready Defense* (Nashville, TN: Thomas Nelson Inc., 1993) p. 308
2 Marilyn Adamson, Connecting with the Divine. 7/12/2007. ttp://www.everystudent.com/features/connecting.html pp. 2-3
3 Ibid., p.1
4 Welcome to Scientology, 7/12/2007. http://www.scientology.org/
5 New Age, 7/12/2007. http://www.answers.com/topic/new-age
6 Other Religions – the big differences, 12/18/2007. http://guide.gospel.com.net/resources/religion.php.

Chapter 28

1. Matthew 27:11-13
2. Matthew 26:63-66
3. Luke 23:13-14
4. Luke 23:20-24
5. Luke 23:23-24
6. Matthew 27:26-31
7. John 19:17-18
8. Matthew 27:35
9. Matthew 27:41
10. Matthew 27:44
11. Matthew 27:40
12. Matthew 27:42
13. Luke 23:39
14. Matthew 27:50
15. John 19:31-35
16. 1 Peter 2:21-25
17. Jon Meacham, Who Killed Jesus? 5/16/2008. *http://www.newsweek.com/id/53129*
18. Luke 24:44
19. NIV Note for Luke 24:44-46, p. 1864
20. Isaiah 53:3
21. Matthew 20:18-19
22. Psalms 22:16
23. John 15:25
24. Exodus 10:1-2
25. 1 Corinthians 15:3
26. Romans 6:6
27. Chadwick, Henry, *The Early Church* (London: Penguin Books, 1993) p. 15
28. Ibid., p. 21

[29] Ibid., p. 22
[30] Diaspora Ii.- The Scattering. 5/16/2008. *http://www.israelmybeloved.com/channel/historyprophecy/section/diaspora_ii*
[31] Chadwick, Henry, *The Early Church* (London: Penguin Books, 1993.) p. 171
[32] Ellerbe, Helen, *The Dark Side of Christianity* (Orlando, FL: Morningstar and Lark, 1995) p. 70
[33] Ibid., p. 50
[34] Crusades, 12/30/07. *http://flholocaustmuseum.org/history_wing/antisemitism/crusades.cfm*
[35] Anti-Jewish Myths Evolve in the Middle Ages, 12/30/07. *http://flholocaustmuseum.org/history_wing/antisemitism/crusades/cfm*
[36] Economic Factors Contributing to Hatred of Jews in the Middle Ages, 12/30/07. *http://flholocaustmuseum.org/history_wing/antisemitism/crusades/cfm*
[37] Deuteronomy 14:2
[38] McDowell, Josh, *A Ready Defense* (Nashville, TN: Thomas Nelson Inc., 1993) pp. 209-210
[39] Exodus 32:6-9
[40] Acts 13:44-46
[41] Romans 11:25-32
[42] Will, George, "Fear of Film Disregards Larger Menace." *The Washington Post*, 8/31/04
[43] Zion Oil and Gas, Inc.-The Joseph Project, audio, 5/17/2008. *http://www.zionoil.com/*
[44] David Krusch, Christian Zionism, 5/17/2008. *http://www.jewishvirtuallibrary.org/jsource/Zionism/christianzionism.html*
[45] Eschatology, End Times, and Millennialism: Competing Theories, 5/17/2008. *http://www.religioustolerance.org/millenni.htm*
[46] David Krusch, Christian Zionism, 5/17/2008. *http://www.jewishvirtuallibrary.org/jsource/Zionism/christianzionism.html*

Chapter 29
1. Elvis Has Left the Building. Dir. Joel Zwick. Writ. Mitchell Ganem, Adam-Michael Garber. Perf. Kim Basinger, John Corbett. Capitol Films, 2004.
2. Paul Simon, Graceland. From the album "Graceland," Warner Bros. Records, Inc., 1986
3. Strobel, Lee, *The Case For Christ* (Grand Rapids: Zondervan, 1998) p. 192
4. Ibid., p. 212

Chapter 30
1. City of Angels. Dir. Brad Silberling. Based on "Wings of Desire." Writ. Wim Wenders, Peter Handke, Richard Reitinger, Dana Stevens. Perf. Nicholas Cage, Meg Ryan. Atlas Entertainment, 1998

Afterword
1. Matthew 6:6

About the Author

C. William "Chet" Galaska was born in 1951. He began his college education at Drew University in Madison, NJ and graduated from the University of Hartford, West Hartford, CT with a Bachelor's Degree in Business Administration. He was president and co-founder of a company producing stainless steel and high alloy castings for industrial applications that grew into a multi-million dollar enterprise. In 2003, he sold his interest in the company and now invests in real estate.

His credentials are defined by what he is not. He isn't a theologian, Ph.D., pastor or philosopher. He's a person who was an unbeliever, influenced by the same things as other skeptics, who became a Christian after several years of investigating the faith with an open mind. This book is a down-to-earth explanation of what he learned.

He played rugby, earned a Private Pilot's License, is a Certified Scuba Diver, has skydived, likes roller coasters and enjoys traveling.

He and his wife Lisa live in Western Massachusetts.

CPSIA information can be obtained
at www.ICGtesting.com
Printed in the USA
LVOW13s1614210318
570660LV00013B/697/P